From Cowtown to Desert Metropolis

From Cowtown to

Whitewing Press

Desert Metropolis

Ninety Years of
Arizona Memories

ROY P. DRACHMAN

Whitewing Press
P.O. Box 65539
Tucson, Arizona 85728-5539

Distributed by the University of Arizona Press, Tucson.

Library of Congress Catalog Card Number: 99-62482
ISBN 1-888965-02-9 (cloth)
ISBN 1-888965-03-7 (paper)

Title page photo: Downtown Tucson, 1946, probably from "A" Mountain. The Pioneer Hotel (*left of center*) was the tallest building in town. *Courtesy of the Arizona Historical Society.*

Contents

CONTENTS

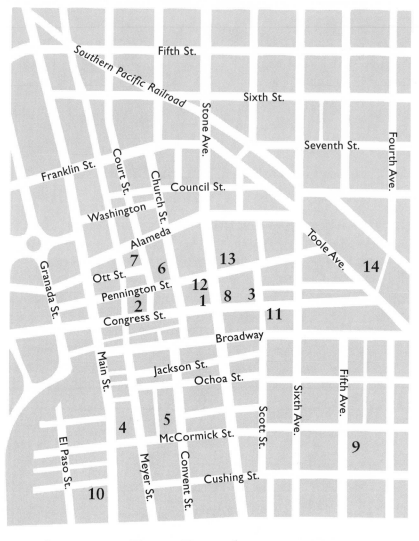

Roy Drachman's Tucson
Downtown in the 1930s

1   Fox Theater
2   Lyric Theater
3   Opera House
4   Drachman Main St. House
5   Red Light District
6   Court House
7   City Hall
8   Litt's Drugstore
9   Safford School
10 Elysian Grove
11 Santa Rita Hotel
12 Dooley's
13 Pioneer Hotel
14 Fourth Avenue Subway

Foreword

You will meet a remarkable man in these pages, a man who has been a major participant in the life of Tucson, and of Arizona, for most of the twentieth century and whose family has helped shape Tucson and southern Arizona since shortly after Arizona became part of the United States. Roy P. Drachman's life began in 1906 in an adobe house on a dusty street in a small, hot, remote western town named Tucson. He was born into a world of vaudeville, buggies, and flickering silent films; he wrote these reminiscences on a laptop computer, as the city he had so much to do with building approached the third millennium as a metropolis of nearly a million people. It's been one hell of a ride, and here he shares some of his best stories from along the way.

As a true gentleman, Roy has been reluctant to spend much time in these stories on what was once known as the "merely personal": his marriages, religious background, and so forth. Being less of a gentleman, I'll mention them here.

Although the Drachmans were Jewish, Roy's mother, the immigrant daughter of a Belgian shoemaker, had been raised Catholic. But Roy grew up in a thoroughly secular environment. He says of that background: "Neither my father nor any of his siblings showed any interest in religion of any kind—why, I don't know. My dad said many times he had never attended services in any church. He believed strongly that all the religion one needed was observance of the Golden Rule: 'Do unto others as you would have them do unto you.' He was a very strong advocate of truth, loyalty, and consideration for your fellow man.

"Several times a Jewish friend of his would attempt to convince him he should send us boys to the synagogue. He made a promise to do so to one close friend. My brother Frank and I were told that we had to attend service there two weeks in a row, but if we didn't want to attend after that, we didn't have to. Two weeks were enough for us."

Having been brought up for a portion of her early life in a convent, Roy's mother had renounced Catholicism before marrying his father. "So," Roy says, "we would attend the church that had the best baseball or basketball equipment. We attended functions at the YMCA and I was a De Molay, a Masonic organization for young men. I got a taste of religion through those activities, but several times I've regretted that I didn't know stories from the Bible."

Though religion may have not played a large part in Roy's upbringing, a sense of the social responsibility that has guided his legendary philanthropic activities was instilled in him early. He recalls that not only were his parents and grandmother responsible for that sense, but also his third grade teacher, a tiny blond woman named Goldie Gibson.

"For some reason," Roy says, "she took a special interest in me. She talked about things no other teacher ever had. She told me she expected me to be better than I had been in learning things. For the first time, she made me realize that I was fortunate to have parents and other relatives in the community who cared about me and my brothers. And that our family was setting an example of serving as important citizens, so that I had a responsibility also to take a place of importance in Tucson someday.

"I remember that one time a Mexican-American boy in our class and I had jointly made the highest grade on something and had won an award. She told me she was giving the prize, a new geography book, to the other boy. She explained that he came from a very poor family that didn't always have enough food or clothing. She made me realize that while our family was poor, I was better off than he was, and that I should feel good about giving up a portion of the award to make the other family proud."

That lesson, which tells us we *are* responsible for others, and for sharing our good fortune, was one Roy learned well. From making sure his mother was comfortably taken care of after the untimely death of his father, to his wide-ranging charitable and civic activities, he has proven himself worthy of those who trusted in him.

In a business career that didn't begin until he was forty, Roy became a wealthy man, primarily through real estate, though early investment in the Price Club via his friend Sol Price improved his balance sheet considerably. In some of these stories you'll come to understand better the economic and civic forces that have shaped the contemporary Southwest, as told by a man who was a major player

Roy with John Denver and broadcaster Dave Sitton at the dedication of the Tucson Boys & Girls Club in Tucson named after Roy.

in that shaping. What makes Roy unique is that as he was fulfilling his role as a developer, he was always motivated not only by personal gain, but by a vision for the betterment of the community. While Arizona in the last fifty years or so has seen many people from outside the state come into it solely in order to profit financially, Roy has been from birth part of the fabric of the city and state. As he has benefited, he has seen to it that Tucson and Arizona have benefited also.

Since Roy is not only a gentleman, but a supremely modest man when it comes to mentioning his good works, I'll happily again be less of a gentleman and do it for him—in spite of his protests.

He is partly responsible for the existence of Tucson's major community hospital complex, Tucson Medical Center, having chaired the fund-raising committee whose success allowed TMC to be converted from the private Desert Sanatorium in 1943 to 1944. And in a happy historical irony, fifty years later, he found himself head of another successful funding campaign for the same hospital, one that made its continuing presence as a community facility possible.

When the University's Arizona Cancer Center needed help on its

Left to right Mrs. Oliver Drachman (Alice), Mrs. Lorraine Drachman, and Mrs. Roy P. Drachman (Sally).

Left to right Roy E. "Manny" Drachman, Boyd Drachman, Roy W. Drachman, and Roy P. Drachman as they are today. *Photo by Carter Allen.*

Drachman family gathering about 1959. *Standing, left to right* Manny (Roy E.) next to wife, Lorraine; Betty Jo and husband, Jim; Joan and husband, Frank E., Jr.; Isabelle; Cowan and wife, Grace; John W. Taylor, husband of Rosemary; Miliana, daughter of Grace and Roy; Helen and husband, Craig; Susan, daughter of Dick and Fanchon; Dick; *seated, left to right* Frank E., Sr.; Phyllis next to husband, Roy; Millie next to then husband, Albert P.; Rosemary Taylor; Oliver next to wife, Alice; Fanchon, wife of Dick.

way to becoming the major national force it is today, Roy stepped up again in 1986. He became the first $1 million donor in the university's history. And shortly thereafter, he chaired the university's Century II Campaign, which raised almost $200 million.

Anyone who today enjoys Agua Caliente Park does so because Roy donated the money to purchase it. Any scholar who works in the Drachman Institute of Real Estate Research does so because of Roy. And students who learn in such diverse fields as architecture, journalism, and creative writing will do so because of scholarships established by Roy, and through bequests from his brother Albert. There is even a scholarship established in the name of his former housekeeper, Elizabeth Brown.

The list goes on. Athletic, civic, professional, social, and educational activities—in all these areas Roy Drachman has been deeply involved and has been in the lead.

Of marriages, Roy has had three. The first, to Grace, lasted twenty-nine years, from 1927 to 1956, and produced Roy's two children, Manny and Miliana. Manny has been in partnership with Roy for thirty years; Miliana is married to a Dallas attorney. Between them, they have given Roy seven grandchildren, and those grandchildren have given him twenty-one great-grandchildren, all of whom are delights to their grandfather/great-grandfather.

After Roy and Grace divorced, Roy was married nineteen years to Phyllis. That marriage, like his first, ended in divorce, though it gave Roy a surrogate daughter in Phyllis's younger child, Kay.

For the past twenty-one years, he has been very happily married to Sally and the two of them make an impressive team, indeed. "Happiness," Roy says, "is all around me."

And it is, without question, a well-earned happiness.

ROBERT HOUSTON
The University of Arizona

Introduction:
A Different Tucson

I SUPPOSE ALMOST every man has wished at one time in his life that his father could come back for a day. You'd like to tell him what you've done since he departed this world and perhaps even show him what's happened to the town where he lived and spent most of his life.

This would be particularly true for me, because my father and I spent practically all of our lives in the same town, Tucson. And because my father died while I was only twenty-seven, and because that was so long ago, sixty-six years, tremendous changes have occurred in our town. I would have a very busy day, trying to tell him about, and show him, what has happened to the village where he was born in 1872, when it had a population of about 3,000 people—and no doubt even more burros, dogs, mules, horses, cats, cows, and chickens than that, not to mention the wild things.

I've thought about being able to have this day with my father many, many times over the years. In imagining what I'd tell him and show him, I've filled a basket full of ideas. And then I've thought about my grandchildren and great-grandchildren, of whom I have twenty-one. I've concluded that one day they also may be interested in some of the things I would talk to my father about.

And perhaps you might be, too.

So I decided to put into my laptop Macintosh, and eventually on paper, what I would talk to my dad about. That's the principle reason I'm writing these articles and vignettes. They represent one man's viewpoint of the changes I've observed here over the last seventy-five or eighty years. The results are not a history of Tucson, because I am not a historian, nor do I want to do the research into exact dates or names required in a historical account of an era or place. My principal hope is that this book will provide an interesting and fairly accurate account of some of the events and people and the roles they played on the Tucson scene during most of the twentieth century.

My two brothers and I always addressed our father as "Pop." So I would say to him, "Pop, Tucson's not the same as when you left us in 1933. First of all, the Depression we were suffering from in 1933 ground on through 1937, although it became less severe as the years passed. In the late 1930s, we began preparing for another world war and the vast expenditures for that war altered your town forever, as they did the nation. I'll show you some of the things that still exist here as a result of those years. We won't have much time to talk about the war, but we won and Frank and I were in the service, as you were during the Spanish-American war *over* a hundred years ago. Remember?"

I'd tell him that, for my part, I well remember what he told me Tucson was like shortly after he was born here in 1872 and while he was growing up, then how it began to change from a small territorial village made up mostly of adobe buildings, few of which were even plastered to avoid the appearance of being mud huts, into a real town. There were no paved streets nor cement sidewalks until around 1910, when Tucson's most important street, Congress, was paved after a close, hard-fought election about such then-dubious progress.

I would say to my father, "I remember you told me that the election was an example of what I would likely experience on many occasions during my lifetime when, no matter how right any idea or issue might be, there would always be opposition to it and I shouldn't allow such opposition to discourage me from supporting it, providing it was quite apparent that it was the correct thing to do. You've proved to be right. No matter what good idea is proposed there are always those who oppose it." Then I'd continue my tale of what he told me Tucson was like during the early days before I was born.

Horses played an important role in Tucson's transportation system then. They pulled its streetcars from downtown to the University of Arizona campus, way out on the east side of town. Horses also pulled the ice wagons, the milk wagons, the wagons delivering eggs and butter to Tucson homes, all delivery wagons, privately owned buggies, public carriages, and fire wagons. Wood wagons driven by Indians from the reservations delivered a cord of mesquite to homes for two or three dollars.

Stables were important buildings in that small, raw town. Nearly all streets had hitching posts. Some business buildings had hitching rails—the parking garages of those days—where several horses could be tied. Water troughs were a common sight. Naturally, the streets had to be cleaned of horse droppings, a civic expenditure we're mercifully free of nowadays.

Vendors with small pushcarts cruised around both business and residential neighborhoods. They hawked *cimarrones,* a shaved ice and fruit syrup treat served in paper cups; *menudo,* a favorite soup and hangover cure among Mexican and pioneer gringo hombres; and tamales served from a large yellow lard can kept warm by hot stones. And there was always that old Greek gentleman selling popcorn from his glass-enclosed cart on the northeast corner of Stone and Congress.

I'd drive Dad down South Main to the spot where our old adobe home stood at 233, an address now vanished beneath the parking area for the Community Center. He might suffer a moment of nostalgia, but I think his spirits would be lifted to see that the old Wishing Shrine, just south of El Minuto Cafe, hasn't moved.

"The Carrillo School is still there on the site of the Elysian Grove which you and Nat Hawke ran," I'd say to him, remembering warm nights at the vaudeville, motion-picture, and amusement-park complex I knew so well as a boy. And I'd have to tell him that Pastime Park on Oracle Road, three long miles from downtown, with all its family pleasures, is also gone.

I would show him that blocks upon blocks of adobe buildings, as well as my childhood home—buildings that made up an important part of the Old Pueblo—have been cleared and are now the location of the Community Center. Those old buildings housed not only many saloons but also Tucson's large, legal, red-light district. (In its heyday, the district accommodated at least 220 prostitutes around an area known as Gay Alley, off Sabino Street. It was a block east of South Meyer Street and north of McCormick and operated until prostitution was outlawed in 1915.)

While we were in the neighborhood, we'd both recall the Chinese grocery stores that provided groceries, vegetables, and bakery goods to most Tucson families. The stores were generally old adobe homes converted by the enterprising Chinese families, who then lived in the back of the buildings.

Dad would surely remember shopping in the few meat markets around town, such as the Young Brothers' on East Congress Street. And we'd both recall Craig's, a familiar grocer also downtown on East Congress. But Steinfeld's, at the northwest corner of Stone and

Pennington, was Tucson's largest grocery store, delivering orders from that location to the homes of families who could afford such service until after World War II.

Steinfeld's was also the largest department store in downtown Tucson—where all merchants were located—though not the only one. There was Jacome's, for example, a smaller store, but one that grew over the years. Then there was the one the Kitt Brothers operated, on East Congress, and Rebeil's, also on Congress just east of Sixth Avenue. Around 1914, Kress, probably Tucson's first chain store, opened next to Kitt's on Congress.

I would show him the vacant lot on the north side of East Congress Street between Stone and Scott and say, "Neither one of us ever thought the Opera House would be demolished and that nothing would be built on that important downtown spot. But there it is."

I would ask him, "Do you remember the time when Brud (my brother Frank) and I had our tonsils and adenoids removed by Dr. Olcott at his office on Pennington, just east of Stone? You called a horse and carriage to take us back home to South Main." Then I'd point out that the doctors' offices downtown, like the stores, are almost all gone, too. I think he'd be comforted to know that St. Mary's Hospital, the largest then, hasn't moved, though it's vastly different. But the Southern Methodist Hospital, which was on North First Avenue a few blocks north of Speedway, is no more. Doctors' offices and hospitals were less central to life then, however: many children were born at home, as I and my two younger brothers were, and doctors made house calls. They all used horses and buggies, until a Dr. Fenner (wasn't he the one, Pop?) around 1914 to 1915 became the first Tucson physician to use an automobile to make his rounds.

Dad had his pick of places to fill Dr. Olcott's prescriptions, all in the downtown area. Litt's Drugstore, operated by T. Ed Litt on the northeast corner of Congress and Stone, was probably the busiest, but Fleishman Drug, a few doors east on Congress, was probably the oldest. (Charlie Winter ran it for the Fleishmans.) Owl Drug was located on the northeast corner of Congress Street and Sixth Avenue, and Economy Drug on South Meyer. All of the drugstores had soda fountains and served soft drinks, ice cream and sandwiches.

Or Dad and I could have tried the Palms Cafe back then, which served light meals just east of Litt's on Congress and was operated by Mrs. Nora Nugent and her family. The Chocolate Shop and the Palace of Sweets, both on East Congress Street, also offered fountain service and light meals. Rossi's, however, on the northwest corner of Congress and Stone, was the most important restaurant in town.

Barbershops were a much more important part of the community during my father's days in Tucson, before the development of the safety razor. I remember that Pop had the straight-edge kind but was afraid to use it, as were most men. Those stainless steel straight-edge razors were dangerous instruments. So nearly all men made daily visits to the barbershops, which also were centers for them to gather and talk sports and politics and to share local gossip.

Dad and I knew several hardware stores downtown. One was run by the Steinfelds, another by the Corbett family—who also operated a large lumberyard—and another by John Ivancovich in a store on East Congress. Steinfeld's was by far the largest and sold heavy equipment to mining operators, though the Ronstadts had a sizable hardware and ranch equipment store on South Sixth Avenue and Broadway, where they also ran a buggy-building operation and blacksmith shop. A related business, which was an important part of the community, was the Jacobs family's assay office, which would evaluate the quality of the ore that a prospector would bring to town from a far-off mining claim he had established somewhere in Arizona or even in Mexico.

In about 1912 or 1913, the streetcar system became electrified, and its lines were extended from East Congress south on Fourth Avenue to Seventeenth Street and west to Main and the Elysian Grove. A few years later, the lines were extended north on Main (past our home) to connect with the West Congress Street line, completing the loop around the south side of town. There were very few automobiles on Tucson's streets until around 1915.

This roughly describes Tucson as Dad knew it up until about 1916, or around the time World War I started. He and I witnessed relatively slow growth—given what would happen later—over the next fifteen or twenty years. From 1920 to 1930, Tucson's population grew from around 23,000 to about 32,000. The first two downtown skyscrapers, the Pioneer Hotel and the Consolidated National Bank Building, went up in 1929. Tucson was beginning to stir a bit and was on the threshold of becoming a modern city, when the Depression hit town.

The Depression put a kibosh on building activity, so there weren't many homes built here between 1929 and 1935. The main activity surrounding homes during those years involved families' trying to keep from losing them because they couldn't make the mortgage payments.

The federal government, under FDR's New Deal, developed the Federal Housing Administration—the FHA—and the Refinance Corporation—the RFC—which enabled many families to save their homes from foreclosure.

But, oh, how all that changed.

I'd drive my dad out east of town, beyond where the development ended before he left us (around Campbell Avenue). I would tell him that what he'll see as we drive east on Speedway is a Tucson that didn't exist at all in 1933. I'm sure it would be difficult for him to believe what happened between Campbell and almost out to the mouth of Sabino Canyon.

"I remember," I would say to him, "that you told me that you had driven a wagon full of supplies and men who had been formed into a posse to try to capture Geronimo and part of his tribe after a raid on a ranch on the east side of Tucson. You said that the sheriff had hired the wagon from your father, who had a hauling business, and that, although you were too young to be a member of the posse, you drove the wagon to Sabino Canyon."

I know that he would find it almost unbelievable that much of the land that had been homesteaded by friends of ours in the late 1920s and early 1930s near Sabino was now covered with homes and apartments. I'm sure he would marvel at all the places to shop without having to go downtown or to a neighborhood Chinese grocery store and at how the houses themselves have changed.

MY DAD WAS always interested in finding a way to cool a house during Tucson's beastly hot summers, without success. During the years he ran the Opera House, he always advertised it as the "Coolest Place in Town," and it was! Many old-timers used to come there two or three days in a row, not so much to see the movie as to sleep in a cool place.

"A couple of years after you left us in 1933, Pop, some smart guy came up with the idea of the 'swamp cooler,' which was successful in cooling a house rather inexpensively, and from that time on, every house in town was cool in the summer months," I would tell him. And that's one reason the houses changed: as a result of the development of swamp coolers there was no more need for the screened sleeping porches that were included in practically all homes while he was still alive.

As our day for Pop's visit would rapidly slip by, I'd tell him that the seemingly endless development he had seen as we drove east on Speedway was also occurring along the main streets and roads farther to the southeast and almost to Vail, which he'd remember as a ranching community some twenty miles east of downtown. Later in the day I would have to show him the equally impressive growth in the northwestern part of our valley, out beyond the old Steam Pump and the Pusch Ranch, owned by his friends of long ago and I would try to explain to him how it all came about.

During the latter part of the 1930s, I'd say, as the Depression was gradually being overcome, primarily because of defense spending by the Federal government, Tucson began to benefit from the establishment of what is now Davis-Monthan Air Force Base and of Marana Field northwest of the city and from the enlargement of Fort Huachuca.

During this period and well into the years of World War II, Tucson and Phoenix experienced solid growth in the tourist business. Both cities aggressively sought tourists, and because the war prevented tourism overseas, it boomed in Arizona. There were 112 guest ranches around Tucson, as well as the El Conquistador Hotel, with its 240 rooms, and the Arizona Inn. There was even a daily Arizona Limited train that operated over the Rock Island and Southern Pacific lines from Chicago to Tucson and Phoenix during the winter months for four or five years.

The war brought thousands of young men and women to Arizona, many of whom didn't realize that the snow and ice they were used to back home didn't exist all over the nation. They fell in love with our weather and many returned to live in Arizona, mainly around Phoenix and Tucson. This, plus the move to Arizona by large companies such as Motorola and Hughes, triggered truly explosive growth during the 1950s. The population in both cities jumped dramatically.

With that growth came the need for all kinds of improvements. Thousands of new homes began to spread across the desert areas in the Valley of the Sun and around Tucson. Large, world-class resort hotels sprang up around both cities. Many wealthy visitors, attracted by those resorts, fell in love with Arizona and, as a result, hundreds of million-dollar homes were built here and in the Phoenix area. Land values soared, and it appears that our dramatic home building will continue for the near foreseeable future.

Tucson became a "university town" over the years, too. Our universities grew tremendously and came to be counted among the nation's largest. They also became recognized as among its best, with the University of Arizona being rated among the top ten public research universities in the country.

I'd drive my father around the campus and point out its many new buildings. I'd certainly show him the football stadium and the McKale Center, named for his friend, J. F. "Pop" McKale. And I'd remind him that he told me he had driven a carriage full of University regents to the groundbreaking for the university's first building, Old Main, which is little changed since then.

At the end of the day, I'd drive Pop past the U of A's huge Health Sciences Center on North Campbell and then on to downtown again, where I'm sure he'd be saddened to see that not only are nearly all the stores and restaurants gone but that even the Old Pueblo Club, where he spent so much time in his later years playing cards with his friends such as Pop Gunst, Pete Martin, Elmer Present, Monte Mansfeld, Hi Corbett, John Reilly, Tex Shelton, and a few others, is no more.

That's not a thought I'd want to leave him with so to show him something I know would greatly please him, I'd drive out to Hi Corbett Field and show him how the ballpark he helped design, and which was built at his urging by the city when he was chairman of the Tucson Baseball Commission, has expanded from a seating capacity of 1,200 to nearly 8,500.

I'D SAY, "POP, I know that you were a nut about baseball all your life but you never saw two major-league teams play a game against each other. Now all Tucson baseball fans get to see many games every spring, since eight big-league teams train in Arizona. You'd have your fill at last." And I'd have to brag that I had something to do with getting Arizona recognized as a good place for major-league spring training and that I've seen over ninety World Series games, many with Hi Corbett, our mutual good friend.

So, while I would have had a wonderful day seeing my father again after his sixty-three-year absence, I'd have to admit that although what has happened to Tucson during those many years is primarily good, it's a long way from being perfect.

Tucson has changed completely from that small village my father knew in the nineteenth century. It also is a great deal different from the town I can first remember, about 1915. It has grown steadily to become what it is today, a city of some 750,000 souls. It may be bigger, and I believe better in many ways, but it was a wonderful place to grow up in, most of a century ago, despite its drawbacks. I'll be telling you about those years, and many others before and since, as we go along in this book. All in all, I'm glad I resisted the urge and opportunities I had to move to some other city during my lifetime.

When you're done reading, you may even agree I did the right thing.

Childhood and Family

A Tucson Childhood

A FEW THINGS keep popping up in my mind about early Tucson. Some of the most warm and enjoyable times I remember were the Drachman family gatherings, either at our home or at the home of one of my uncles, Harry or Mose or Herb (who really was a first cousin of my dad's though we called him Uncle Herb). They were all about the same age—not more than seven or eight years apart.

These gatherings would usually take place in the evening for dinner. They normally included the eight adults and about eight of us older kids, all boys. The oldest in our generation was Rosemary, daughter of Mose, who was generally away at school. She was the only girl in that generation of our family until Rosalie, the last child in that brood, arrived at Uncle Harry's house. So altogether we were ten boys and the two girls who were the first and last born. We boys didn't mind if Rosemary wasn't present because, at that age, we didn't think much of girls yet!

We looked forward to these family dinners. All the ladies were excellent cooks and served delicious dinners and desserts. However, the best thing about these family dinners was to sit around and listen to stories by the four men about the old days in Tucson. We would listen by the hour to the fascinating and funny tales about people and events in the early days. After all, Uncle Harry was said to be the first white child born in Arizona. You can't go back beyond that unless you're Native American or you resort to reading history books, and there weren't many of them about Tucson or Arizona around at that time. We would hate to see the evenings come to an end. We never seemed to tire of the yarns the men would spin.

Sometimes one of the uncles would become philosophical and point out to us boys the responsibility each of us had to uphold the honorable name we bore, which had been established by our grandfather, Phillip, and his brother, Sam, during the latter part of the last century. They had been very involved in establishing the educational system in Tucson and had served on the school board for several years. I guess they figured someone had to educate all the kids they brought into the world, a total of fourteen between them. They were also involved in politics, both having served in the territorial legislature. Harry and Mose served on the school board, and Harry had been both city and county treasurer.

I remember my mother lecturing my brother and me about something that one of us did, stressing that "A Drachman doesn't do something like that," and then telling us again about the importance of never doing anything that might bring dishonor to our name. It made me think about how I had to conduct myself as I grew up, and I think about it still. Neither of my uncles, Mose or Harry, nor my father, went beyond the fourth grade in school because they had to go to work to help support the large family they were part of.

WHEN MY BROTHER and I started playing baseball with other kids in the neighborhood, my father made a baseball for us that was the best size for our small hands. He took a solid rubber ball, such as girls used to play jacks with, and wrapped woolen yarn around it time and time again until it was about three inches in diameter. Then he covered all that with black electrical tape, which kept it from unraveling. It was quite hard and served well as a baseball. I had watched the way my dad had made it, and I made many of them myself over the years. The regular baseballs used in schools and by professional teams were too large for us until we were almost high school age. Besides, they were very expensive, costing $1.25 each!

During those days, we lived on the south side, or the wrong side of the tracks. Most of my friends were Mexican-American kids with whom I had grown up. Our neighborhood was pretty poor, and we kids had few and modest toys compared to what children have today. We played marbles by the hour, spun tops, flew kites, and played baseball when we could get or make a ball and a bat. All our outdoor

Roy, on the right, at
4¹/₂ years, with
brother Frank, 3¹/₂.

activities took place either on the dirt sidewalks or on the dirt streets. We were bothered only occasionally by a passing wagon or horse and buggy.

Even when we moved off Main Street to South Stone Avenue, which was kind of a dividing line between the gringo neighborhood and the Mexican district, I used to go back to my old neighborhood to play marbles or baseball with my old friends. The gringo kids didn't know how to shoot marbles worth a darn and I liked the competitive attitudes of the Mexican-American kids who played much better.

We lived not far from Barrio Libre, which translates loosely as "Free District," a notorious neighborhood where even the police went only in pairs or groups, and which was located along South Meyer Street, only a block south of McCormick Street, where our home was located. Once in a while, some of the roughneck Mexican-American kids from Barrio Libre would drift into our neighborhood, and it often happened that rock fights between our gang—generally made up of our Mexican friends, my brother and me—and the unwelcome visitors would result. I don't remember anyone getting hurt in any of those frequent rock fights. Once, however, several of us were caught by the Barrio Libre gang outside the adobe wall around the Scott yard across Main Street. We were pretty scared of what might happen, because we were outnumbered better than two to one. Walter Scott was in our group that day and his mother, a tough lady, came with a revolver outside of the backyard to where we were, fired a couple of shots in the air, and told the visiting roughnecks to get the hell out of our neighborhood. They retreated posthaste, thankfully permitting our return to safety. We avoided confronting those guys again.

Rock fights were part of everyday life on the south side. We all developed good throwing arms—we had to hold our own. On the last day of the school year, for no reason except for tradition, the gringos and the Mexican kids would have a gigantic rock fight. This would rage up and down the south side streets and vacant lots.

Once, some gringo who had been given a BB gun by his father, went home and got it. Someone called the police, and they showed up and stopped a large part of the fight.

Dallas Ford, the Tucson chief of police, and Jesús Camacho, a detective, responded in a Model T Ford. Camacho was well liked and highly respected by all of us kids. He took the BB gun from the kid who owned it. Dallas Ford was across the street talking with a bunch of kids. He was standing by his car and kind of leaning over with his back toward us. Camacho aimed the BB gun at Ford's rear end, an inviting target, and fired a BB that made Ford jump but didn't really hurt him. Camacho acted as if he hadn't done a thing and was facing away when the chief looked at him. Anyway, the rock fight was broken up without further ado.

Living on that side of town, we gringos soon learned some dirty, insulting signs that the Mexicans used when facing an unfriendly fellow. One of them was the "*toma* sign," which was made by folding your arms, facing the adversary, pointing your fists at him, and then pulling your arms back to your body. As you did that you yelled, "Toma," which means "take this." Another dirty sign used by the Mexicans to tell someone off was made by forming a "V" with your thumb and your forefinger, turning the back of your hand toward your adversary, and then taking the forefinger of your other hand and pointing it through the "V" at the other guy. It was customary for the person to whom the insult was directed to respond in kind.

In June of 1924, after our Tucson High baseball team had won the Arizona state championship, we were invited to go to San Diego to play a series of three games versus San Diego High, which had won the California state championship. It was a great trip and good experience, although we lost all three games. On the way over, the train on which we were traveling entered Mexico on two occasions. Several of us were sitting at the back of the observation car and, as it traveled slowly along the tracks in Mexico, we passed two or three work crews. Someone in our group made the "*toma* sign" at them. Immediately they dropped their picks and shovels and returned the favor. Of course, we thought that was great fun and we repeated it a few minutes later as we passed another work crew. Its members' response was the same. It was much more important to return the dirty sign to us than to keep working. We laughed every time this happened.

But after the train got back to the United States, the conductor came to us and showed us a telegram he had been handed containing a message from a Mexican railroad official complaining about the insults directed toward the Mexican workers. The conductor said if it happened the next time we entered Mexico, which was a few miles down the tracks, we would be ordered off the train in Mexico. That straightened us up in a big hurry!

WHILE I WAS living on South Stone Avenue, the United States was involved in World War I, and during that period the Spanish influenza epidemic was sweeping across the world. One measure adopted to curtail the spread of the disease in Tucson was to avoid having close contact with other people. The local schools decided that there should be more space between school kids. This was accomplished by making sure there was a vacant seat beside each kid, which was, in turn, accomplished by having all classes meet for just half a day. I was in a class that met only in the afternoons. This schedule went on for most of the school year, giving me free mornings to do all kinds of things from selling morning "extras," released daily at 11 A.M. by the *Tucson Citizen*, to building and flying kites. But for me, the most fun was building a small, one-passenger race car with much assistance from a Mexican-American boy whose last name was Olivas.

I always used only that name, Olivas, as he had asked me to, and in fact I never did know his first name, although we spent a great deal of time together building and racing the car. He lived just a block north of our home on Stone Avenue in an old adobe house. His father worked at the Southern Pacific shops to support the family, which included three other children, one of whom was Jimmie Olivas, a good baseball player with whom I played many times ten years later.

My friend was a year older than me and was a good-sized kid and quite heavy, but hard as a rock. He prided himself on his ability to run and push me in our push mobile. I tried to get him to take turns in riding and pushing, but he insisted that I be the driver and he, the provider of power, or the pusher.

Olivas was also on a school schedule with mornings open. He spent all morning at our place working on the push mobile in our garage, which was not used because we couldn't afford a real automobile until a few years later. We started with a set of wheels from an old buggy we acquired from a friend. Olivas was a quite capable natural mechanic, and it was he who designed our car and provided the know-how to build such a thing. He even came up with a method to provide a braking device.

We spent the better part of a month building it, painting it, and getting ready to race other kids on the south side of town. We had ball-bearing wheels, which most of the other push mobiles lacked, thereby making our vehicle roll easier and faster, especially with the great power behind me in the person of my buddy, Olivas. We would race up and down South Scott Street in front of where the Temple of Music and Art is now. There was little traffic on Scott, so it was ideal for push mobile racing, which we did on weekends.

Another thing Olivas and I did was build extra-large kites. I was the expert on kite making, but we worked closely together. We liked to fly them on windy days during those winter and spring months when there were usually very high winds, using heavy, strong string. On two different occasions, when the wind was blowing in the right direction, we connected the string from the kite in the sky to the front end of our push mobile and used the kite as an airborne sail. It actually worked!

Olivas devised a pulley with a large hook on it, which we could hang from the kite string while the kite was aloft. Once we attached large sheets of wallpaper, four to six feet long, to the hook. The heavy wind would blow them aloft, all the way along the string to the kite itself. Olivas figured out a way to shake them off the hook when they

The Drachman family about 1915. Emanuel (Manny) and Millie holding Albert, and Frank (*left*) and Roy standing behind them.

reached the kite. Today we'd be arrested for littering: those large sheets of old wallpaper dropped from the sky all over the south side of town. When the hook and pulley were freed of their load very close to the kite, they'd come whistling down the string at sixty miles an hour and provide great excitement for us and our friends, who would usually gather to watch us fly our giant kite.

WE THREE BOYS—my brothers, Frank, who was seventeen months younger than I was, and Albert, who was six and a half years younger, and I—enjoyed good health most of our lives. The only serious illness I ever suffered came when I was almost a year old and the family doctor told my parents that I had to be taken to the West Coast. He didn't believe I would survive the summer's heat. My mother and I went to Long Beach, California, where we stayed with one of my father's

The Drachman boys, Albert, Frank, and Roy, in one of the last photos of them together.

sisters for the balance of the summer. My mother was then carrying her second child, Frank.

Frank's only major departure from good health was a bout with pneumonia when he was six. Albert, likewise, was healthy most of his life except for a serious illness, scarlet fever, which he contracted when he was eight or nine years old. He nearly died, and I believe, as did our doctor, that if it hadn't been for the valiant efforts of my father and mother to save him, he would not have survived. We two older boys moved over to my Uncle Mose's house for two weeks because our home on Fifth Street was quarantined. Scarlet fever was a highly contagious disease for which they had none of the sophisticated serums available today.

Albert was running a high temperature, which the doctor said could be reduced only if he could be made to sweat. My father was determined to make that happen. He took the round lids off of the wood-stove in the kitchen after they were very hot, wrapped them in news-papers and then in a damp towel. They were placed under Albert's back, on his stomach, and on his chest. My father also heated bricks and similarly wrapped them and placed them between Albert's legs and along both sides of his body. He kept that up for two days and nights. It worked: Albert did break into a heavy sweat. His fever was broken and the crisis passed.

My mother enjoyed good health until she was quite old, but my father was not so lucky. After his forty-fifth birthday, it seemed that he always had one health problem or another. In 1917, he had an appendectomy at the old St. Mary's Hospital, which did not go through the usual healing process. Dr. Arthur Olcott, his physician and a good one, called it a "puss case," his term for an infection of the blood that was very serious. Dad finally began a slow recovery, but he was confined in the hospital or at home for well over a month. It seemed that he never was as well as he should have been for the rest of his life. He suffered from a form of rheumatism called "break bone fever" (though it is properly called dengue) by some old-timers. He also had "stomach problems," which required him to take powders that came in folded thin white papers from the drugstore and which had to be stirred into a glass of water. The doctors thought he had an ulcer.

He wasn't allowed to eat Mexican dishes containing chili, which he loved as much as we boys did, and which my mother cooked so well. He later developed "heart trouble," about which the doctors knew very little at that time. When he was fifty-three, he had a heart problem so serious his doctor told us on Thanksgiving morning in 1925 that he didn't believe he would be alive at Christmas.

That was a sad time for our family, although we never told Dad what the doctor had said. Anyway, as a result of that news, I decided I had to quit school and immediately go to work managing the Rialto Theater. I dropped out of college after only one year and a couple of months. I started working on the Monday after Thanksgiving in November of 1925 and have been working ever since. Fortunately, my father lived for another eight years, but he was never very strong.

Rosa Drachman and Some Memories

EIGHTY-THREE YEARS ago, I spent nine months living with my paternal grandmother, Rosa Drachman, in Santa Monica at the old Kensington Court, which still stands there on its bluff overlooking

Mother Rosa Drachman (Mrs. Phillip) sits with her ten children at Kensington Court in Santa Monica, California, in 1915. Nine of the brood were born in Tucson, Mose in San Francisco. They are, *left to right standing,* Harry, Becky, Emanuel, Lillian, Mose, Esther, Minnie, and Albert P.; *sitting,* Myra, Mother Drachman, and Phyllis.

the beach and ocean. Mother Drachman, as she was referred to by many friends in Tucson, was a very hardy soul, the mother of ten children, nine of whom were born in Tucson.

She was widowed when my grandfather, Phillip Drachman, died at the age of fifty-six, one year after his youngest child, Phyllis, was born. Rosa had to find a way not only to support her children but also to raise them. The three oldest were boys who had been already working for several years to help support the family. They had little education. My father dropped out of the fourth grade when he was ten to help his father, who was in the freight business, hauling all kinds of things across the desert from Yuma to Tucson and on to Lordsburg,

New Mexico. He used twenty-mule teams on the long trips, but he also had a local hack, or taxi service, which my dad worked at even before he quit school.

My grandfather also owned a small clothing store, had a saloon for a while, and did a lot of contract work for the cavalry unit stationed in Tucson, cutting wild hay in the desert in places where there was enough rain for it to grow.

One time he and a partner had a haying crew working about ten miles north of town. They were attacked by Geronimo and his fellow Apaches. The crew's foreman was killed, the wagons and horses stolen, and the men roughed up. My grandfather and his partner sued the government, claiming that they should have been protected. The suit dragged on for several years, during which time my grandfather died. Eventually, his side won the suit and received a paltry amount, part of which was paid to Rosa.

She told me that my grandfather had first come to Arizona in 1854, the first year that southern Arizona was owned by the United States as a result of the Gadsden Purchase agreement with Mexico. In that purchase, all the land south of the Gila River to the present border was acquired for $10 million. The U.S. Congress approved the purchase on December 30, 1853, so my grandfather was here within a year after it became a territory of the United States. He didn't establish his residency here until 1860, however.

Phillip had come to the United States from Poland with Barry Goldwater's grandfather and great uncle, as a trio of youngsters trying to avoid service in the Russian army, which, at that time, ruled Poland. The three boys were smuggled out of Poland and eventually came to America on the same steamer in the late 1840s or early '50s. The Goldwaters went on to California while my grandfather went to Philadelphia to work for a relative in a tailor shop.

But the lure of gold mining was strong and it was reinforced with mail from the Goldwaters. Finally, it became irresistible and Phillip sailed for California around Cape Horn. The trio remained in California, but over time the three moved into Arizona. I have a copy of a census report that listed one of the Goldwaters as a resident of Tucson around 1860, but they eventually established themselves in Prescott and then Phoenix. A few years ago, Barry Goldwater said that no town in Arizona was large enough for both the Goldwaters and the Drachmans, so his family chose Prescott and the Drachmans chose Tucson.

Phillip's brother, Sam, two years younger, took ship from Poland to a port in the southern United States and remained in that area for a few years. He served in the Confederate army, then, when the Civil War ended, came to Tucson to join Phillip. Sam established a dry goods store and, after a while, opened a cigar store and pool hall on a prominent corner in the downtown area. It became a popular gathering place for years.

Phillip and Sam became involved in local politics, and each served in the territorial legislature. Sam sat for several years on the Tucson School Board. He outlived Phillip by quite a few years, not dying until 1911. I remember seeing him just once, when my mother and I walked home from the Opera House, which my father ran at the time. We stopped by Sam's cigar store, and I remember that he picked me up and stood me up on one of his pool tables. He gave me an old pool ball, a number 8, which afterward I kept around the house for years. I was five years old.

In 1868, my grandfather Phillip decided he needed a wife, and he set off for New York City to find a lady to become his soulmate. Louie Zeckendorf, who lived in New York and who was one of the Zeckendorf family that owned mercantile stores in Santa Fe and Tucson, knew Phillip. Phillip had worked for Zeckendorf for about a year in the family's Tucson store. Louie was my grandfather's contact in seeking a bride. Uncle Louie, as he was known by friends as well as family members, introduced him to one of his cousins, a young lady from Baltimore by the name of Rosa Katzenstein.

Within a few weeks they were married and set sail for California via the Isthmus of Panama, which they crossed in a horse-drawn wagon. They eventually reached port in San Francisco, then sailed down to Los Angeles. From there, they traveled overland to San Bernardino, the home of my grandfather's younger sister, Augusta. She had come to America after he had and married Hyman Goldberg, who also was from Piotrokov, Poland. Augusta and Hyman later moved on to Phoenix, where they raised a large and successful family of merchants who operated the Goldberg store.

Phillip and Rosa's marriage was in the early part of the summer, and Phillip feared that his bride from the East Coast would not endure the terrific heat of the desert very well, so Rosa stayed in San Bernadino with the Goldbergs while he went ahead to Tucson. He returned for her in the fall, and they commenced a twenty-five-day trip by wagon for the Old Pueblo. They arrived in early November. There

22

Roy's paternal grand-parents, Phillip and Rosa Drachman.

was only one other Anglo woman living in Tucson at the time, my grandmother said.

She told me the trip across the desert that first time was very difficult. She said they encountered the worst kind of rough men. They passed graves of many earlier pioneers and were constantly fearful of Indian attacks. To avoid the heat, they traveled at night. The few saguaro cacti without arms that they passed frightened them because as they approached the silhouette they never knew if it was an unfriendly man or a saguaro.

The life of a young American woman in Tucson was far different from the one Rosa had become accustomed to, living in a large port city like Baltimore. None of the homes had indoor plumbing, and none of the first few of my grandmother's Tucson's homes even had wooden floors. She soon adapted: she had to if she wanted to raise a family and be a good wife to Phillip. She became an active housewife, mother, and member of Tucson's social life.

Her first child, Harry, was born on February 3, 1869. He later claimed to be the first Anglo child born in Arizona, which seems a little far-fetched but, as far as I know, no one has seriously disputed his claim. He was so proud of his heritage, in fact, that he adopted "Arizona" as his middle name and had it properly and legally recorded. He was known as Harry Arizona Drachman for fifty years, until his death in 1951.

Rosa was busy for the next few years adding to Tucson's population by bringing nine other children into this world. The next ones, after Harry, were Mose and Emanuel, who was my father. Of the following seven, only one was a boy: Albert. It seems strange, but only the three oldest boys had children. And only the three men with fam-

Harry Arizona Drachman, Tucson City Treasurer, 1903.

Roy's Aunt Lillie and friends in patriotic garb in the 1890s. *Top row,* Ruth Strauss, Lulu Katzenstein, Trecia Montoya, Etta Goldtree, Bernice Cheney. *Middle row,* Ruth Brown, Emma Johnson, Bernie Culver. *Bottom row,* Lillie Drachman, Florence Fish, Lydia Roca, Ina Wilkinson, Beryl Richardson.

ilies remained in Tucson, while the others moved to southern California. Rosa followed in 1908 or 1909 and settled in Santa Monica, where she lived until her death in July of 1918.

During those nine months I stayed in Santa Monica with her, one of her daughters, Lillie, and her youngest son, Albert, she told me about her life in Tucson and in Baltimore before she married my grandfather. One of the many things I remember her telling me about was her experience of watching the funeral procession of Abraham Lincoln.

That procession, with its somber official party and black hearse, had made a lasting impression upon her, as it probably had on everyone in the large crowd she said was assembled on the streets of Baltimore.

At the time she told me about seeing the funeral procession, it was just fifty-one years after Lincoln's assassination. It seemed to me then to have happened sometime far, far back in history, and yet today as I am writing these notes, over fifty-one years have passed since the end of World War II and the date I was mustered out of the army in 1945. It doesn't seem to be very long ago at all.

The House in Which I Was Born

I WAS BORN in an adobe house at 233 South Main Street on the northeast corner of Main and McCormick. Every house in the neighborhood was built of adobe. I lived in that house until I was ten years old. It seemed to be a large house to me, although it really wasn't.

When Main Street was built, it must have been cut out of a dirt hill because all the houses on the east side of the street sat on a bluff about eight or ten feet above the level of the sidewalk. A stairway rose from the sidewalk up to our front porch, which extended across the entire front of the house. There were rocking chairs on the porch, though we seldom used them.

There was also a porch at the rear portion of the house that was rather small in my first memory of it, but which was increased in size by a carpenter my father hired to build a screen porch large enough for four or five beds. My brothers, Frank and Albert, and I slept there every night, summer and winter, stormy weather or fair. There were canvas curtains that were rolled up most of the time but which were used to shelter us from the rain. When the wind blew while it was raining, we often had sprays of water hit us. Nearly every house in Tucson had screen porches that people slept on in the summers and some families, like mine, also had children sleep year-round on them because it was said to be healthy for growing kids.

Sleeping on the screen porch on cold winter nights wasn't much fun, but after a few minutes in a bed with adequate quilts and blankets we slept soundly. We didn't have many childhood illnesses, so I guess it wasn't harmful in any way. I never slept inside regularly until I got married at the age of twenty.

A hallway led from the front door at the center of the house to the

Calle Real (today South Main Avenue) in 1895. It was part of King's Highway running from Mexico City through Alamos and Tubac to Tucson. The first house on the right, 233 South Main Street (at the northeast corner of Main and McCormick Streets), was first the home of Rosa Drachman, then in 1905, of Emanuel and Millie Drachman, and the birthplace of their three boys: Roy, Frank, and Albert. Beyond it was the home of Teofilo Otero, and beyond that of Colonel Stevens, where Roy met Buffalo Bill (see page 32).

back porch. There were four rooms along the hall. The first one on the left was the parlor, and the first one on the right side was the bedroom where our parents slept.

One of my most vivid memories of many, many years ago is of sitting on my mother's bed in my parents' bedroom in the house on Main Street. We were looking at a picture in the newspaper of a big new ship, the Titanic, as it was preparing for its first trip across the Atlantic to New York City.

My mother read the article to us about this unsinkable ship, made of steel, that had just been launched. She had to explain to my brother Frank and me how a ship made of steel could float because we knew that steel came from iron, which was very heavy. A few days later, we

Roy at twenty-three months.

heard that this unsinkable boat had actually sunk before it completed its first trip.

I also remember sitting on her bed looking at pictures in the paper of German soldiers with strange hats that, she explained, were helmets made of metal, worn to protect them from bullets. The soldiers were shown with machine guns on tripods. We knew something about those because one of our boyhood heroes, Pancho Villa, had machine guns, too. The picture in the paper was accompanied by an article about the beginning of the First World War in Europe, although, at the time, no one knew it would develop into a war that would involve many of the world's nations, including our own.

My mother was very interested in the war stories because the Germans were again fighting the French. She had been born in Paris and had many cousins in Belgium where her father came from.

The second room on the left of the hall was a small dining room, and the last room on the right was the bathroom. It had been added sometime after the house had been built.

The hall led to the back porch, which was a couple of stair steps below the level of the hall. To the rear of the dining room there were also a couple of stair steps down to the kitchen. A door off the kitchen opened onto the back porch, which ran along the side of the rear portion of the house. In back of the kitchen was another bedroom, which also had a door to the back porch. At the rear of that back bedroom was a storage room in disrepair—it was at the very rear of the house and part of the rear wall was missing.

The house was quite old, having probably been built in the 1870s. My grandmother had bought it soon after her husband, Phillip Drachman, died in 1889, and said it was the first house she'd had in Tucson that didn't have dirt floors. She and my father were living in it when my parents were married in 1905. All of my father's other nine siblings had flown the nest. My father and his bride, Millie, moved in with my grandmother, who, in 1910, herself moved to Los Angeles to be with several of her daughters who had gone there earlier because there were few jobs for young women in Tucson.

There was no electricity to the bedroom at the rear of the kitchen and on the rare occasions when we used it, we lit it with oil lamps. The other rooms in the house had two wires running along the middle of the ceiling from which a single lightbulb hung. There were no light switches near the doors; you had to reach up and turn on the bulb by hand. Needless to say, the quality of light was not good a few feet away from the lightbulb. We often supplemented it with oil lamps.

There was no heat in the house and, of course, no cooling. In the winter, we boys would move our clothes in the morning to the kitchen to dress in front of the stove whose open oven threw out some heat.

The large, flat-topped iron stove burned wood. If we wanted to eat, we boys were expected to keep the wood box next to the stove filled. The kitchen was large, containing a table on which my mother prepared food, a couple of easy chairs, and a table on which we ate most of our meals. Of course, there was also a sink and a small ice box. The ice box had space at the top for the cake of ice that would be delivered as needed from the horse-drawn ice wagons on their daily rounds.

Our kitchen was where we spent an awful lot of time. We boys studied and did our homework there because in the winter months it was the only place in the house that was warm enough to be comfortable. I remember looking over my father's shoulder as he read the paper in that kitchen and telling him I knew what "that word" was, pointing to "the," which is the first word I remember being able to read.

It seemed that my mother was in the kitchen all of the time, cooking bread twice a week—quite a chore—or preparing one meal or another. We would watch her mix the dough for the bread, knead it, put it in the individual loaf pans, apply a bit of lard over the top to make it shine, and then set it out to rise before putting it in the oven to bake. It was also fun to watch her roll dough and slice it into long noodles, which we all loved. She used some of the dough to make delicious doughnuts as well.

For breakfast we had either rolled oats or cream of wheat, which my mother taught me to fix in the early mornings before school. We never had eggs and bacon, because it was probably cheaper to serve the cereals. I'm glad we didn't eat eggs because I didn't like them.

For dinner we never had such a thing as a steak; I was a pretty big kid before I even knew what a steak was. We often had pot roast with mashed potatoes and gravy, although I never cared for gravy. Mexican frijoles were a staple for us—I loved them then and still do! I remember we had a nice Mexican lady who would come once or twice a week to help my mother. Her name was Carmen, and she was a good cook. She wanted us boys to eat beans at least one meal a day, telling my mother that "The boys won't grow up to be strong men unless they eat beans every day."

I remember my father teaching me how to spin a top on our kitchen floor by winding heavy twine around it, holding it upside down, throwing it toward the floor, and pulling back on the string just as it reached the floor. It took a couple of nights, but I finally learned the trick.

Because the house sat on a relatively small lot—41 feet wide and 138 feet deep—there were no windows on the north side of any of the rooms. The house next door on that side was cheek by jowl with ours.

Along the south side of the backyard a white picket fence ran from the house to the end of our lot, which backed up to a Chinese grocery store. In the yard there was usually a pile of mesquite logs replenished from time to time from one of the Indian wood wagons that cruised the streets in those days. We boys were expected to use the hatchet or ax to cut the wood into pieces small enough to fit into our kitchen stove.

Another chore we boys were responsible for was emptying the pan under the ice box where the water from the melting ice dripped—usually a daily duty. Because our ice box was not very large, we bought many food items from the Chinese grocery store, Suey Yen's, almost every day. One of us would go to the store for our mother. It was a chore we liked because Suey Yen would always give us *pilón,* which was usually a couple of jelly beans or a couple of peanuts. That was a custom around Tucson in those days—like the stamps given by many grocery supermarkets later on.

In our backyard, a row of pomegranate trees, which produced a good crop of enjoyable fruit, grew just inside the picket fence. We were expected to regularly water them and pick their fruit, much of which we gave to neighbors.

None of the streets was paved, nor did any have cement sidewalks or curbs along them. When it rained, they were a muddy mess, particularly the sidewalk along McCormick, which was largely caliche, a gray kind of dirt that is very slippery when it's wet.

Across from us on the west side of Main Street, there was a row of adobe houses occupied by Mexican-American families. All of those houses had dirt floors, and none had indoor bathrooms. They were occupied by very nice families and two of the boys, Robert Woods and Armando Martínez, were my best friends. I hated to leave them when we moved away. Robert and I remained good friends all of our lives, although when he got married he moved to a ranch just south of the border in Mexico and I seldom saw him after that.

There were only three other gringo families in our neighborhood. The George Atkinson family lived across McCormick Street in a house that had been built and occupied by the Albert Steinfeld family before they moved to their home on North Main. The Will Scott family lived in the adobe house across Main from the Atkinsons. A Colonel Stevens and his family lived one house removed from us to the north, on the east side of Main.

George Atkinson was a rancher, and he owned the first automobile I ever saw, which was around 1910. It was built much like a horse buggy and had an engine under the seat that had to be cranked from the driver's side of the car.

Will Scott was a retired judge who was confined to a wheelchair all the time I knew him—he was a crotchety old guy who drank a lot. He was married to Larcena Pennington, whose family had been killed by Apache Indians in a famous incident several years before. The Apaches had left her for dead but she survived terrible wounds and was found and returned to Tucson.

Scott Street was named after that Scott family and Pennington Street after the Larcena Pennington family.

Colonel Stevens was a retired army officer and a friend of Bill Cody, better known as Buffalo Bill. Once, as I mention again later, when Buffalo Bill came to Tucson with the Barnum and Bailey Circus, he visited Colonel Stevens. Colonel Stevens invited my brother Frank and me to come over and meet the famous man.

The neighbors on Main Street were the only part of the neighborhood that was good. On the corner of Meyer and McCormick, there were two Chinese grocery stores and two saloons (which weren't very classy joints).

Just a half block east of Meyer Street on McCormick was Tucson's red-light district, known as "Gay Alley," where a host of prostitutes lived and conducted their business.

I attended kindergarten run by Mrs. Schrader, a doctor's wife. The school was located on the northwestern corner of Stone Avenue and McCormick Street, just four block east of where we lived. I was only four years old, but I remember quite a few things about that little school. It was the first place I remember being taught by anyone except my parents. I recall, too, that we had to walk up McCormick right past Gay Alley, which is discussed further later on, both going to and coming from school every day. At night it was not uncommon to hear men and women screaming at each other as they had their drunken parties and fights in the middle of the night.

A couple of years later, I commenced attending public school at the old Mansfeld School on South Fifth Avenue. I remember we walked up to my Uncle Harry's home on South Sixth Avenue, just one block west of the school house, and picked up my cousin, Byron Drachman, who was the same age, and then were taken by our mothers to the first day of school.

That was eighty-eight years ago. The school building still stands and is being used as a part of the Safford School.

ONE OF THE good things about living at 233 South Main was that it was only a block from my father's amusement park, the Elysian Grove (which I recount in more detail in "An Old Tucson Tradition Sadly Lost"). We would visit the Grove on many evenings. We would roller-skate at the skating rink, have a lemonade at the beer garden, or watch live performers who appeared at the outdoor airdrome on occasions. With the coming of Prohibition, the Grove was closed and sold to a real estate developer, who created a residential development there. The Carrillo School is located on the east end of the Grove property.

We moved from Main Street in 1916 to a house on South Stone. I hated to leave that old house and my friends on Main Street. I remember that I left my baseball bat in back on the hall door so that I could have an excuse to visit it one more time. It seems like only yesterday that I walked through the house for the last time, the time I went there alone to get my bat.

The house was torn down around 1920 and another adobe house was built there, which was, in turn, demolished when the Community Center was built. The site is now the southeast corner of the parking area for the center. Main Street has completely been changed through that part of Tucson. The vacant fields, known to us as *milpas,* that once spread out at the rear of the houses on the west side of Main Street have been developed as building sites or are roads. Nothing remains.

Some Unforgettable Family Events

I'M SURE THAT all of us have unforgettable family events that cause us to smile a bit when they pop into our minds. I have a couple that involved my brother Frank, known to all of us as "Brud." He was only a year and a half younger than I so we were quite close while growing up.

He often had nightmares and would sometimes walk and talk in his sleep. One of us in the family would have to wake him and return him to his bed, none the worse for the experience.

While we lived in a house on the southeast corner of South Stone Avenue and Fourteenth Street, we always slept outside on a screened porch. One night, at about one o'clock, Brud jumped out of bed, unlatched the screen door, and started running across the backyard.

I yelled to my dad that Brud was having a nightmare and took off after him. By then he had jumped a low fence, crossed the street, and was running north, heading for Scott Street. He passed the home of my father's partner, Ben Goldsmith, who happened to be sitting on his lawn on that hot summer night.

As we ran past Ben and his teenage son, I yelled that Brud was having a nightmare and asked them to join in the chase. We ran past the vacant lot where the Temple of Music and Art is now and finally caught up with him as he was heading up the walkway to the library. I grabbed and shook him. He was wide-eyed but still half asleep. He said he had to return a book to the library.

My dad and the Goldsmiths arrived just in time to start the trip back home. We all had a good laugh as we walked home.

On another occasion, Brud had a major nightmare at our home on Fifth Street. It happened soon after I'd gotten married and, while I didn't witness it myself, my father told me about it.

Brud had moved into the small, second floor screen porch where I used to sleep. It was up a flight of stairs off the large screen porch, where my father was sleeping. On this occasion, Brud let out a loud whoop and came down the stairs, excitedly saying, "Someone is shooting at me!" He was ducking up and down, acting like he was hiding behind something. He continued down to the floor of the lower screen porch where he tried to kick one of "them." Instead, he kicked the wooden area under the screen.

He suddenly woke up, in considerable pain. The next day, his big toe was swollen. He went to the doctor, only to learn that he had, indeed, broken his toe trying to kick his imagined assailants.

Another humorous event I remember occurred one summer when a large crate of crab apples arrived, addressed to my mother. They were sent by our Aunt Ethel, Mrs. Mose Drachman, from California. My mother remarked how thoughtful it was of her to send such a nice gift.

My mother was a great cook. She made a couple of pies, which we thoroughly enjoyed, and a tasty pudding and then she gave some of the fruit to a neighbor lady. In any event, we used all of the crab apples.

A couple of weeks later, Aunt Ethel returned to Tucson and called my mother to see if the fruit had arrived. My mother thanked her for the nice gift and told her how much we had enjoyed the pies and the pudding she'd made. However, Aunt Ethel was quite upset. She knew that my mother often preserved fruits during the summer months, even though it was very hard work, especially in a very hot kitchen with no air conditioning. She had sent the fruit expecting my mother to preserve the fruit in jars for her!

My mother explained that, because there was no note attached to the box of fruit, she thought it was a gift to her. We had a good laugh about the whole episode because we had enjoyed the fruit so much and thought it was pretty nervy of Aunt Ethel to expect my mother to put up the fruit for her.

In 1919, when we were still living on South Stone Avenue, my father bought his first automobile. Naturally, it was a black Ford with seats for two in front and three in back—just right for our family.

It became a custom, every summer evening at about nine-thirty after my father had finished his duties at the Opera House, for him to pick us up and we'd all go for a drive. We'd drive north on Stone and out on Oracle Road, which was the only paved road outside of the downtown area. It was paved to the bridge over the Rillito River, which we would cross, then turn around and drive back home.

We boys would sit in the back and often take a nap. One night, Brud and I got to scrapping and disturbing our parents. We were told to quiet down. When the ruckus continued, my father said that if we started again, he would stop the car and make us walk home. Well, we continued to cause problems and, sure enough, he stopped the car and told us to get out. We were out by the cemetery and it was pretty dark.

We started walking, but soon a car came along and stopped. The driver was a man we both knew. When we told him what happened, he told us to hop in and he'd drive us home. He was a good friend of our father's and thought it would be fun to get us back home before our parents arrived.

Indeed, we did arrive home before them and were sitting on the front porch when they pulled up to the house. Naturally, they were very surprised to see us. Both of our parents were laughing as they asked us how we got back and so soon. We all joined in a good-natured round of kidding, but we learned one thing—that our father meant what he said when he threatened to make us walk home!

A Bomb Attack and My Boyhood Jobs

In 1916, while I was in the fifth grade at the old Safford School on South Fifth Avenue, an enemy of the Aros family dynamited their home, which was located on the south side of East Fourteenth Street, just west of Fifth Avenue. Even though it was the middle of the night, we heard the explosion at our home a couple of blocks away. Rumors were that the Aros family had enemies from Mexico who were responsible for this act.

Luckily for them, no one was seriously injured. Most of the force of the blast was directed toward the street and nearby neighborhood.

The old two-story Safford School was about a half block away. The blast blew out several of the windows and shook the building so badly that it had a gap along the southwest corner from the ground, clear up through both floors.

Nonetheless, the building was examined by architectural engineers and deemed to be habitable. They draped a canvas over the damaged corner and propped up the walls with large timbers so that none of the students would be injured in case there was any movement, and we continued to attend classes there.

During the following summer, the building was torn down to be replaced by a new school, which is the Safford School that stands on that site today. As the building was being demolished, it was decided that the red bricks from it could be used again for the construction of the new building. The bricks had a lot of mortar on them, and the builders employed several of us youngsters to clean them.

I remember that I used a Boy Scout hatchet which, of course, was completely ruined by chopping the mortar off the bricks. The other kids and I had a gentlemen's agreement among ourselves that none of us would steal bricks from the other. For cleaning those bricks and piling them up in neat forms, we were paid all of one cent per brick. We could clean about fifty or sixty a day. I remember that I cleaned over three thousand bricks that summer and was paid a grand total of thirty-seven dollars, which was not too bad for a ten-year-old kid back then.

That was just one of the jobs I had as a youngster. I used to distribute handbills in Tucson's residential areas for my father's theater every Saturday and Sunday, for which I made fifty cents per week.

I learned how to make kites, too, and would sell them for ten cents apiece. They would take me about an hour to make, and I believe I didn't charge enough for them. I also set pins at the bowling alleys at the YMCA, which was quite a hazardous job. The pins would fly wildly when they were knocked down, especially when they used the duckpins, which were only about eight inches high.

I also sold newspapers. The highlight of that career was selling the *Tucson Citizen's* War Extras, which came out every day around eleven in the morning except on Sunday. We would buy our papers from the *Citizen* and run up and down the main streets of Tucson, yelling, "War Extra, War Extra!" We paid two cents for the papers and sold them for a nickel, making seventy-five cents to a dollar a day. That was a lot of dough for a kid of Boy Scout age.

And I trimmed trees. I would climb up one with a special little saw and trim the branches off so that it would have good growth the following year. I did that for two or three years. I also had a job watering lawns. I was paid two dollars a week per lawn; each lawn had to be watered seven days a week.

During that time, I also had a route delivering the *Saturday Evening Post*. I had over thirty subscribers. I had a special canvas bag that I wore over my shoulder, big enough for all thirty-odd copies of the *Post*. It was a good-sized magazine, so thirty copies made a heavy load to lug from house to house.

When I went to high school at fourteen, I took a regular job ushering at the old Opera House, which was owned by my father and Ben Goldsmith. I worked six nights a week from 7:00 to 10:30 P.M. and was paid five dollars a week.

However, out of that five dollars, my father said that I had to pay three dollars per week to my mother for my room and board. Once I paid for my room and board, I was left with two dollars. In those days, that was a pretty good amount for a high school kid. But I can guarantee you that I ate more than three dollars' worth of food a week, so it was a good bargain!

World War I and Tucson

IN 1916, WHEN Woodrow Wilson was running for reelection, posters around town all proclaimed, "He Kept Us Out of War." World War I had been going on for about two years at that time and many people were afraid that the United States was going to become involved in that European war.

At the time, my father was chairman of the Pima County Democratic Party, and my brother and I helped distribute window posters for Wilson. I remember going into a barber shop on East Congress Street and asking the owner for permission to put a poster with Wilson's picture on it in his window. He told me, forcefully, what I could do with the poster. It was the first time I had ever heard that expression and I never forgot it.

In the months before the United States became involved in the war, strong feelings were building against Germany, which was very aggressively challenging most of Europe with its strong desire for lebens-raum, land area for expansion of the German people.

The newspaper accounts of an interview between the German ruler, Kaiser Wilhelm, and U.S. ambassador Gerard stirred up strong anti-German sentiment, for example. In them, the Kaiser is said to have claimed that Germany had 50,000 spies in the United States, to which Gerard was said to have replied, "Well, we have 50,000 lamp-posts to hang them from."

In 1916, Pancho Villa led a large force of his followers across the border to raid Columbus, New Mexico, during which two American citizens were killed and considerable supplies stolen.

The entire nation was up in arms over the incursion. Congress de-manded that President Wilson respond aggressively, which he promptly did by sending a U.S. expeditionary force under the command of General John "Black Jack" Pershing into Mexico to run down and punish Pancho Villa and his banditos. Villa was never found, but he never again stepped on U.S. soil.

All of this further stirred up concerns about the possibility of Ger-man spies' penetrating our country from Mexico, which had, for years, been one of the most popular places for German immigrants to settle.

Of course, Woodrow Wilson was reelected and, not long after that, the United States entered the war. I was ten years old, and the idea of a war was a very exciting thing. Soon after that I became a member of the only Boy Scout troop in town. We were involved in quite a few wartime activities, one of which was to accompany the newly trained troops, who arrived weekly at the new El Paso & Southwestern Railroad station on West Congress from Camp Harry J. Jones in Douglas, on their march to the Southern Pacific station at the east end of Congress. A Civil War veteran, Major Neustetter, would organize the troops and lead us and them up Congress Street. Then the troops would board a Southern Pacific train en route to an-other military base. It was a great experience and an exciting one for us. We were part of Uncle Sam's army!

After the United States entered the war General Pershing was given command of all the military forces sent to fight in Europe.

The United States was quickly put on a full war basis. Every man between the ages of eighteen and thirty-five was required to register with their local draft board. Training bases were established through-out the country. Camp Stephen D. Little was set up at Nogales and trained only black troops. At Camp Harry J. Jones in Douglas, white troops were given preliminary training before being shipped to other bases via Tucson over the new El Paso & Southwestern that ran from El Paso to Tucson and then on to San Diego. The line had been built in the years 1915 to 1916.

To help finance the vast military expenditures, several series of war bonds were launched and widely promoted. The Red Cross was seeking not only funds but also supplies such as bandage rolls, which were put together by dozens of female volunteers in Tucson and other towns everywhere.

Special movies based on war themes were released by Hollywood—one of the most popular being "Over the Top," starring Guy Empey. Irving Berlin was turning out wartime tunes such as "Over There."

Airplanes were quite new, and their use in war hadn't yet been proven. However, DeHaviland planes, made in England, were seen over Tucson once in a while: I remember lying on my back on our front lawn watching a daring pilot doing aerobatics several thousand feet in the air and dreaming of someday piloting a flying machine.

I remember, too, being in the old Opera House when the movie was interrupted and the house lights were turned up. Soldiers stood at every exit while men moved through the audience requiring each young man of draft age to show his registration card in an effort to apprehend "slackers."

During the winter of 1917 to 1918, the worldwide Spanish influenza epidemic, which I mentioned earlier, swept across the nation, causing thousands of deaths and heavily striking the armed forces in camps and bases everywhere. Civilians were required to wear white gauze masks whenever they left home. Schools were suspended or went on half-day schedules so that every other desk could be left vacant to avoid spreading the flu. We all had it, mostly mild cases, but there were some deaths here, too.

In the fall of 1918, rumors about Germany wanting to end the war began to circulate. By early November, the rumors had become more persistent, and plans to celebrate victory were quietly made. When the announcement was made that an armistice would begin on November 11, all hell broke loose, with every bell and whistle in town going off for twenty-four hours. Cars raced up and down the streets, and everyone went a little nuts. Prohibition had gone into effect nationally during the war (although it had already been in effect for several years in Arizona), but it became apparent that for a few days lawmen were allowing celebrants a little leeway.

In the big parade a few days later to officially celebrate the ending of the big war, somehow I promoted a ride in a big army tank that was in Tucson for a few days. It was quite a thrill, despite the fact that the ride was a very rough and noisy one.

A few months later, a memorial fountain was built on the campus of the University of Arizona in memory of those Arizona alums who perished during the war. At the dedication, General Pershing, the hero of the U.S. forces, made the principal address. Lawson Smith, my lifelong friend, and I were in the Boy Scout troop that participated in the ceremonies. We were lined up in front of the platform from which General Pershing spoke and had to stand at attention during his entire speech. The newspaper the next day reported that, because of our strict adherence to duty, we stood at attention and never even got to look at the great general. The reporter didn't know that before the ceremony, we each had a chance to shake General Pershing's hand.

Streets of Early Tucson

BACK IN THE early days of the twentieth century before 1915, there was only one paved street in Tucson: Congress Street. It was, by far, the most important business street in the city. Main Street also had many businesses along it, but they were primarily within the first block north and first block south of Congress.

Meyer Street, south of Congress, had many businesses along it, too, until it reached McCormick, which was also known as Thirteenth Street. South of McCormick, Meyer had a few business enterprises but deteriorated rapidly into what was known as Barrio Libre, where lawlessness prevailed, including gambling, prostitution and other nefarious activities. It was said to be the district where criminals lived and hung out, and it was no place to be after dark. It was Tucson's toughest neighborhood, the city's most notorious district.

Congress Street, even before it was paved, was the town's number one street. In the early days, before the railroad reached us, Congress was known as Calle de la India Triste, which translates as "Street of the Sad Indian Maiden." Where that name came from was unknown to any of the old-time Tucsonans with whom I spoke.

The Sam Drachman cigar store at Stone and Congress, sometime after 1920. *Arizona Historical Society.*

Congress was our first paved street, but paving it became a hot political issue, from what I was told by my father and one of his brothers. It was very narrow and divided down the middle by what was known as the "Wedge," which ran west from Stone Avenue to Main Street. My great uncle, Sam Drachman, had a cigar store and pool hall on the eastern tip of the wedge, which made it the hottest location in town. It was a gathering place for politicians, gamblers, and businessmen.

The streets on both sides of the wedge were narrow and dusty, except when the rains came and turned them into muddy messes. The dirt sidewalks were no place to walk when horses splashed mud on them.

Despite the terrible conditions, there was strong opposition when the paving of Congress was proposed and put on the ballot. Opponents claimed that horses would slip and fall if the street were paved and that it would have to be swept daily to pick up the horse manure that normally became part of a dirt street.

Those favoring paving won a tight election and, after the wedge was removed, Congress Street became Tucson's first paved street. Soon thereafter, South Meyer was paved. All the other streets in Tucson remained dirt, with no sidewalks or curbs.

Around 1917, Oracle Road was paved as a two-lane cement road extending north from the intersection of Drachman and Main to the new bridge across the Rillito River. From the bridge north, although it was the only route to Florence, Phoenix, and the West Coast, the rest of Oracle remained dirt. That cement strip of Oracle was the only paved road outside the city limits of Tucson for many years. All of the other county and state roads were two-lane dirt ones, dusty when dry, and dangerous and slippery when rains came.

Few corners had street signs. None had street lights, although over the middle of a few intersections, a lone street lamp hung, strung on lines from corner electric poles. There was such a light at the intersection of Main and McCormick, where we lived. It was a gathering place for us kids during the warm evenings where we would play games, sitting in the middle of the street. There was little danger because there were no automobiles and only a few wagons after dark.

Most of the neighborhood kids were Mexican-American and were our buddies, both girls and boys. We'd play "Run Sheep Run," or a Mexican game, "Colores," or spin tops, or play marbles and hide-and-seek. Telling ghost stories was also a favorite pastime.

A common sight on Tucson streets were the "Indian wood wagons," drawn by one or two horses, driven by an Indian from one of the reservations, and loaded with of a cord of mesquite logs. He would drive through the residential streets shouting, *"leña,"* Spanish for firewood. The price for a load was usually two or three dollars. Every family had hatchets or axes to cut the wood into lengths that would fit into the wood stoves found in nearly every kitchen.

Also seen were Mexican hombres with one or two burros carrying a small stack of short mesquite logs on a cargo saddle. The driver would also shout, *"leña"* to attract buyers in residential neighborhoods.

Along Meyer Street and Congress Street and near other business areas, it was common to see a Mexican fellow making and selling *cimarrones,* paper cups of shaved ice with fruit juice poured over them that sold for a dime. He would push along a small handcart with a large chunk of ice on it that he would shave with an instrument similar to a wood plane. Four or five kinds of juices were available to flavor the cool delight.

In the business districts along Meyer and Congress, there were many small businesses, quite a few operated by moms and pops, selling food products and small, handmade items of clothing and leather. Nearly all of the stores along Meyer were run by Mexican-Americans, because most of the residents were Latino families. We were one of the few gringo families living in the neighborhood.

Early mornings it was common to see a small, four-wheeled cart pulled by a hardworking hombre with a twenty-gallon yellow lard can on it containing a kettle of menudo. This hot soup concoction, containing tripe, hominy, and a few other special ingredients, was a favorite among old-timers including my father, who would stop the vendor and have me get a pot of it for his breakfast. The menudo was kept warm by large heated rocks around the kettle, and the enterprising vendor would loudly announce that the menudo wagon was in the neighborhood.

Other people pulled similar carts with large tin containers full of hot tamales, hawked in residential areas to the cry of "Tamales. Tamales."

Several people drove horse-drawn wagons, delivering various things needed by housewives. Milk wagons were a common sight. A man by the name of Vinson, with his two sons, Harold and Tom, delivered butter and eggs right to your door a couple of times a week. Most ice boxes were too small to store more than a couple of days' supplies of such perishables.

One of the vehicles seen daily (except Sunday) was the ice wagon, drawn by a pair of horses. Two men worked those wagons, which were full of large, 300-pound chunks of ice the men would cut into the proper sizes with their sharp ice picks. Each household had a card with four numbers on it that indicated the size of the piece of ice wanted that day. If they wanted a fifty-pound chunk, they placed the card in the window with the 50 at the top, and the ice man would cut the right-sized piece, bring it into the kitchen, and put it in the ice box.

In the sixth and seventh grades, some of us kids used to wander around on our way home from school. My family had recently moved from the south side of town to the southwest corner of Fifth Street and Fifth Avenue, but I continued to attend class at the new Safford School on South Fifth.

One interesting attraction for me was that the big fire house was not only the headquarters for Tucson's Fire Department but also the stables for the beautiful dappled black-and-white horses that pulled the large fire wagon containing the steam boiler that powered the high-pressure fire hoses. Many times, we excitedly watched those horses run up and down South Main Street, pulling the steaming boiler along "like sixty" as they exercised the horses on that wide street with very little traffic. The fire men were a friendly lot, and we enjoyed visiting them and looking at the large horses. I well remember Fire Chief Roberts as an important hero, in our opinions.

The fire house is still in its original location on South Sixth Avenue, just north of the Tucson Library Park and East Twelfth Street. At the north end of that block on Sixth was the large property comprising the Ronstadt Hardware Store with its wagon- and buggy-building operation and blacksmith shop. It was run by Fred Ronstadt, one of the original Ronstadts, who had lived in Tucson nearly all of their lives. Fred Ronstadt was the grandfather of Tucson's famous singer Linda. The "village blacksmith" had a great deal of historical lore, and though there were several blacksmiths in Tucson, the numero uno for us was Ronstadt's. We'd go there after school and watch them build the various pieces of equipment Ronstadt's customers had ordered. One of the most interesting things to watch was the wagon and buggy painter, putting his artistry to work creating fancy-colored buggies with the pinstriping that only a master could do.

POLICE ON HORSEBACK were often seen, although most cruised in buggies. Horse-drawn "hacks," with a driver sitting above and in front of a cab containing seats for four passengers, were the taxicabs of the time. Horseback riders could be seen everywhere, and there were hitching posts in front of many businesses, especially saloons, barber shops, gambling joints, and, of course, the houses of prostitution along Sabino Street, also known as "Gay Alley."

There were many saloons in the business districts, generally supported by men only. As one would expect, there were some fancy ones catering to upper-crust patrons, while others were less fancy and some were nothing more than dives.

There were two or three good restaurants. Some were run by Chinese or Greeks, others by Mexican families, but the favorite café was Rossi's, which I mention elsewhere.

A common sight on Tucson streets in almost every part of town, including all residential districts, were corner Chinese groceries. They were small stores, in back of which the family lived, and were an important part of the fabric of Tucson life. Nearby residents relied on these small stores for much of their daily grocery needs. Most provided charge accounts on a weekly basis because many of the shoppers were youngsters sent to pick up some things for a mother and didn't bring money.

The Chinese stores did not generally sell meat, leaving that to a few meat markets located along Meyer Street, Congress Street, and in one or two larger grocery stores in the downtown area.

At one time, before 1910, there was a horse-drawn streetcar service that went no faster than a person could walk. Soon, however, electric streetcars appeared on newly laid tracks along Congress Street, along Stone Avenue running north to University Boulevard (then Third Street), and then east to the entrance of the University.

A little later, service was extended from East Congress south along Fourth Avenue to Seventeenth Street, then west to Main Street to the entrance of the Elysian Grove, my father's popular recreational area. Around 1915, the line was extended north along Main Street from the Grove to connect with the line on West Congress. We were living on Main Street when the line was built, and there was a large neighborhood celebration the day the first streetcar came down the new tracks.

Automobiles began to appear on Tucson streets around 1915, just before World War I. They were a rarity for two or three years, but it wasn't long before everyone wanted one, held back only by the costs. By that time, streets were being paved and sidewalks installed. Tucson was moving into the twentieth century—only about twenty years late.

Another memory relating to transportation has to do with the University of Arizona in the decade of the 1920s, while I was either attending the school or following the activities on the campus that involved friends of mine within a few years of my age. I remember that at one Homecoming a captured streetcar ended up in front of the Aggy Building on Sunday morning. This, despite the fact that the end of the car tracks was located where they are today, on Third Street just west of the main entrance to the U of A. Some celebrating college men stole the car from the motorman, and with sheer manpower, pushed it through the campus to where it was found Sunday. Someone had put a large "For Sale" sign on top of it, which they had taken from some property offered by a local real estate broker.

The stolen streetcar was one of a small fleet that operated between downtown Tucson and the campus. It weighed several tons, and getting it back on the tracks was not easy nor inexpensive for the streetcar company, which at that time was the local utility company. It attracted great crowds while on the campus and caused much hilarity for all who saw it. I imagine there must be a photograph of the wayward streetcar because a picture of it appeared in one of the local newspapers as I recall. This was about 1922 or '23.

In those years it was traditional for Homecoming to be celebrated by a large rally including a march to downtown by several hundred students led by the university band. A large bonfire on the campus was where the rally started. Each fraternity house had the pledges gather wooden and cardboard boxes and other inflammable material from around the town for several days during that week to assure a large bonfire. The pile of stuff to be burned would be fifteen- or twenty-feet high and would create a large fire around which the band, the cheerleaders, and the students would gather before heading for the downtown area. At the rally the football coach and some of his staff, and perhaps one or two of the star players, would give short speeches in order to work up enthusiasm for the next day's game.

Show Biz

Show Biz Memories

BEING EXPOSED TO "Show Biz" for the first thirty-three years of my life has left me with many fond memories.

When I was a child, my father owned and operated the Elysian Grove, a popular amusement park of the day. Included in its attractions were a baseball park; a beer garden; Tucson's first swimming pool; a sizable pavilion used as a skating rink, a dance hall, and a movie theater; and an outdoor "airdrome," which boasted a theater with a stage, an orchestra pit, and a projection room, which doubled as the lighting booth for stage productions.

At the early age of eighteen, my mother, Millie Royers, was a professional singer living and working out of Los Angeles, and my father was seeking a single act in the form of a female singer. In response to a request through a theatrical booking agent, my mother, with her rich contralto voice, was booked to come to Tucson to perform at the Elysian Grove in the summer of 1904. The next summer, she returned. And that fall she and my father, Manny Drachman, were married.

I was their oldest child and was exposed to the life of a show business youngster from the get-go, although my mother didn't appear as a professional performer after her marriage. Our old adobe house on South Main Street was just a block north of the Grove. I can't remember when I first started walking there, but I know that I had become a baseball fan, a skater, and a distributor of programs at the theater from the time I was four or five years old.

I remember roaming around the Grove with my dad as he visited various buildings as part of his day's work. I recall his telling me to touch a wire or any other potentially "hot" metal object only with the back of my hand—never with the palm, because the live electricity would cause my hand to curl up and grab the object and give me a serious burn or shock.

As I got a little older, my brother Frank and I used to watch the acts that were appearing in the stage shows rehearse. We got acquainted with many of the performers who would play the Grove for two to four weeks in the Tableau performances, or "Tab" shows. We also knew the musicians, the projectionists, the stagehands, and those who ran the skating rink and the swimming pool—even the bartenders who worked at the saloon and beer garden.

My father said several times that he would not allow me to learn to play any instrument nor to become a musician or a performer or a projectionist. He always said that if we wanted to work in show business, we belonged in the front or business office and not in any other activity. Nonetheless, I do remember one of the performers, a male dancer, taught me a jig step I could do for many years afterward.

The good days of the Elysian Grove were largely confined to the summer months, and by 1915, the advent of Prohibition in Arizona, combined with the problem of declining income, caused my dad to have to close the Grove for good.

He and a new partner by the name of Ben Goldsmith built the Broadway Theater on the southwest corner of Stone Avenue and Broadway. It was a cheaply built frame and metal movie theater with about 500 seats, but it provided an opportunity for my dad to get on his feet again. I worked every weekend delivering handbills throughout Tucson's residential areas, advertising the week's movies.

A couple of years later, he and Ben Goldsmith took over the operation of the Opera House, which not only was a movie theater but also had a full stage, orchestra pit, and dressing rooms equipped to handle the traveling road shows that usually played one-night stands in places like El Paso, Tucson, and Phoenix. Such shows, which were booked out of New York City a month or so in advance, would arrive by train with their stage sets, drapes, performers, and usually an orchestra conductor.

There was great excitement when these shows hit town.

One of the most popular ones to play the Opera House was Arthur Hockwald's Minstrel Show, which came through every year for a two-night stand. This all-black show had a cast of some great performers, many of whom graduated to Broadway and Hollywood. The company

48

of some fifty or sixty people included a group of fine musicians who not only played in the orchestra pit, but would dress up in band uniforms and put on a concert in front of the theater before parading around the downtown, waking up the community and advising one and all that Hockwald's famous minstrels were in town and were performing that very night at the Opera House.

I remember Arthur Hockwald as a colorful man of about five feet six inches and 125 pounds. He was a snappy dresser and well respected by all the members of his company. He always carried a bank roll that would have choked a horse—actually about $5,000, when that amount of money was a fortune. He paid his people in cash because he never stopped any place long enough to open a bank account. Besides, the performers wanted cash, not checks.

From the time I was a youngster of ten or eleven years, I would hang around the Opera House and watch the orchestra rehearse and the stagehands hang the sets and drapes, then go about my job of handing out programs to those entering the theater.

When I was fourteen, I became a full-time usher six nights a week and kept at the job all four years I was in high school. During the summer months after my second year, I worked full-time in the office as assistant manager and relief box-office cashier. I would close the box office, make out the payroll, deposit the money in the Consolidated Bank in the mornings, make out the showtime schedules, and pay the bills. This duty allowed my dad and Ben Goldsmith to leave town during the hot months.

I was getting a liberal education in "show biz."

In 1922, the Rialto Theater was turned over to my dad and his partner, who made a deal with Rickards & Nace, theater operators from Phoenix and the original lessees of the Rialto when it was opened in 1920. I began working there in the fall of 1924 as doorman; at the same time I became a freshman at the University of Arizona.

In November of 1925, I dropped out of school because of my father's health and became the manager of the Rialto. This theater had a much larger stage than the Opera House and seated a couple of hundred more people. From then on, all the road shows—and there were many on the circuit—would play the Rialto.

Appearing there during the late 1920s were such performers as the Sistine Choir, which consisted of some eighty men and boys from

Rome. They packed the theater for two nights and a matinee, as did the Hungarian National Chorus, who entranced the audiences with voices so marvelous they sounded like a giant organ.

One of the most memorable companies that appeared at the Rialto was a Russian one that performed the Boris Goudinoff opera. Naturally, the work was sung in Russian, which, of course, few Tucsonans understood. Near the end of the performance was a death scene, followed by an epilogue.

The Tucson audience, as did those of us working there that night, thought that the death scene was the final act. The audience, or at least 95 percent of them, got up and left the theater after the death scene. In a few minutes the curtain went up and the performers began singing the epilogue. They soon discovered that they were singing to an empty theater. Some of them realized that their Tucson audience was too ignorant to know the show had not ended and broke out in loud laughter, but others carried on for the few moments left in their opera.

The next day the newspapers had a great time poking fun at Tucson's poorly informed opera lovers.

Another Russian performer, the ballerina Anna Pavlova, also played the Rialto with her company of Russian dancers, and thrilled local devotees of ballet. Galli Curci, the well-known star of the Metropolitan and Italian opera, equally thrilled opera fans—who gamely carried on after the Boris Goudinoff debacle.

The world-famous pianist from Poland, Jan Paderewski, played the Rialto and provided a less-than-satisfactory performance. He had a little dog that traveled with him and his wife, who waited for him backstage with the little pup while he played. During his performance the dog barked so loudly that it could be heard by the audience, so Paderewski interrupted his concert to attend to it. This was the man who had been at one time prime minister of Poland.

Each year, a road company of the Broadway show, the George White Scandals, was brought through Tucson by a producer named George E. Wintz. In 1925, the first of these shows played the Rialto. The company was composed of nearly 100 people, including some 30 beautiful chorines. I remember taking mail backstage and down to the dressing room. When I went into the large chorus dressing room, there were about fifteen totally naked women and others in various stages of undress. They were the first naked women I had ever seen and my red, blushing face caused them to laugh at me no end.

In order to assure that none of the girls would jump the company when they hit the West Coast, Wintz bought each of them a mink coat, which would be left on deposit in New York. If and when they returned there, they could pick up their new fur jackets.

About once a month the Rialto offered local theatergoers one of these live bills.

One performer who made an annual visit to Tucson was an old-time trouper, May Robson, who usually appeared in a lighthearted comedy show. She was a local favorite who could always be counted on to fill the Rialto's 932 seats.

Harry Lauder, the legendary Scots performer, would play Tucson every year. His records were enormously popular, and his songs and patter entranced audiences worldwide for years. The last three or four years of his career, he would come through in his "farewell tour," which got to be a joke. He always dressed in Scottish kilts and sported a collection of crooked wooden canes, his trademarks.

In 1926, the Junior Orpheum vaudeville circuit was formed in Chicago to send five-act vaudeville troupes West to one-night stands in small cities such as El Paso, Tucson, and Phoenix. Every Wednesday morning for three or four years, these troupes would arrive at the Southern Pacific station where I would meet them and walk them across the street to the Rialto. I could spot the vaudevillians a mile away when they alighted from the passenger cars. They just dressed differently.

Once settled, they would rehearse with the orchestra, which would be required to play music to fit their acts. Then they'd put on three performances a day: a matinee and two evening shows, at seven and nine-thirty. We would include a second-rate movie with them, but the theater was packed each evening because local audiences were starved to see live acts.

The Rialto had a seven-piece orchestra, which played every day for the silent movies. Such movies continued to be the standard bill of fare for theaters throughout America until the later part of 1928.

By then, Hollywood was feeling its way with sound. At first the production companies were a little timid, not sure that the public really wanted "all-talking" movies. They made "40 percent talkies," then "75 percent talkies," before finally realizing that moviegoers were not only willing to accept sound movies but insisted on them.

With the coming of sound, actors who could not speak lines well were on their way out, along with vaudeville and theatrical orchestras. Thousands of musicians lost their jobs or had to move to Hollywood or New York to find work in the studios.

Show business throughout the world was changed forever with the coming of sound movies.

Even More Show Biz Memories

AROUND 1927, WHILE I was managing the Rialto, the world's tallest man spent a couple of weeks in Tucson visiting his brother, Ben Erlich, who had entered the University of Arizona the year that I did, 1924. Jake Erlich was eight feet six inches tall and had been traveling with the Barnum and Bailey Circus.

Jake spent a lot of time with me at the Rialto during his short stay. He enjoyed meeting people and would stand with me near the entrance to the inner lobby of the theater. I knew nearly all the patrons who came in the theater and, as they first entered the lobby, I would whisper their name to Jake who would greet them by offering his hand and addressing them by their first name. Folks got a big kick out of being greeted by name by this huge man. We had a lot of fun for a week or so while he was here.

Doctors had predicted he would not live past thirty and, unfortunately for this very nice guy, they were right.

An old showman by the name of Louie Mueller moved to Tucson from Ohio in about 1927. He had two aunts who had come here a few years before and owned the old Aguirre Apartments on South Sixth Avenue. They apparently had money, but Louie Mueller never saw much of it while they were still alive.

Louie began hanging around the Rialto and showing up nearly every day, visiting by the hour, telling about his experiences while he ran theaters in New York, Pennsylvania, and Ohio. He was always chewing tobacco, as did many men in those times. We all had spittoons or gaboons, as they were sometimes called, in our offices. My dad frequently chewed a plug.

Louie was, without doubt, the tightest guy I ever knew; he just hated to part with a dime. One time when he was obviously suffering from a serious tooth problem with a badly swollen jaw, he visited three dentists, getting bids on what it would cost to have the tooth removed.

About 1932, during the depths of the Depression, a "sex show" played at the Rialto. By then, my dad had sold his interest in the theaters to the Paramount-Publix theater chain. My boss was Harry Nace from Phoenix, who had also sold his theaters to the same company.

This "sex show" featured a Dr. Diefenbach who was billed as a "sexologist." The show's company included eight beauty contest winners from around the country—a Miss Wisconsin, a Miss Baltimore, a Miss Illinois, and so on. The good Dr. Diefenbach would array the ladies on pedestals on the stage and use a pointer to identify the various peculiarities of the body of each girl, which he said would indicate to a close observer traits of each of them.

There was even a special Ladies Matinee, which sold out the theater. The whole show was a gimmick, of course, but that was what the public was looking for in those tough economic times.

What I remember most about that show company occurred late one night after the show. Harry Nace, Stewart Cash (who was the owner of the show), and a couple of us had a snack at about midnight. Two hours later, Stewart Cash had a heart attack that took his life. His wife was one of the beauties appearing in the show, but the show played as scheduled the next day: the show did, indeed, have to go on.

One of the most interesting and exciting times at the Rialto came during the winter and spring of 1933, when the Wilbur Cushman Revue presented what were known as "tab show revues." The group played three nights a week at the Rialto, and in Phoenix, four.

They put on a completely new program each week. The company included a chorus of six girls who could not only dance and sing but play roles in some of the comedy acts, too. Also, there was an ingenue (a pretty young lady with a good voice), a male tenor, a male and female dance team, a couple of comics, and one or two other performers. They all worked hard. In the mornings they rehearsed and built and painted new sets. Everyone in the company had to pitch in. During the Depression, any kind of job was a good job.

Wilbur Cushman and his wife worked night and day to keep their company of very talented people together. One of the dancers was Hermes Pan, who, with his sister, formed a dance team. After the Cushman show folded, Hermes Pan moved on to Hollywood, where he became one of its very best choreographers, doing nearly all the Fred Astaire–Ginger Rogers classics.

Other annual visitors who would stop by for a visit were the parents of a youngster by the name of Mickey Maguire, who had been featured in a series of popular two-reel comedies. The family later changed the boy's name to Mickey Rooney. Mickey's mother and step-father raised him, although he and his father, an old vaudeville per-former named Joe Yule, remained quite close. Joe had a strong influ-ence in Mickey's career.

I remember during the afternoon or evening when his family would visit me, Mickey would always ask, "Mister Manager, can I go in to see the movie?" Of course, my answer was always yes. Mickey, who was about seven or eight years old, would go down and sit in the front row and watch the movie for as long as his parents were with me. Sometimes he saw the same movie more than once. He must have been studying the screen actor's technique, I guess. He became a fine actor himself and probably has the longest career in Hollywood's his-tory, having starred as a child, as a romantic hero in many Metro Goldwyn Mayer movies, and, more recently, as a character actor in all kinds of Hollywood and Broadway productions.

Years after I left the Rialto, on several occasions when I visited my close friend, Nick Nayfack, a producer at the MGM Studios, he and I had dinner with Mickey and his manager, Harry Friedman, then went for a night on the town with them. I told Mickey about his vis-its to Tucson, all of which he said were just part of traveling the coun-try with his mother and stepfather. He was a picnic to be with and much fun. He was never "off camera"—he put on an act wherever we went—but that didn't keep him from being a genuinely nice guy.

The Fox Theater Era

DESPITE BEING AT the Fox Theater during the Depression years, I found my stint as manager there, starting in 1933, to be cer-tainly one of the most enjoyable times of my life. I was fortunate to be earning, for that time, a good salary plus bonuses.

The first six months at the Fox, which was located on the north side of Congress, west of Stone, were no bed of roses. I was not hired by the division manager of the Fox West Coast Company but by Char-les Skouras, the top official for that company on the Pacific Coast. Tom Sorreiro, the Arizona manager, resented the fact that his boss had hired me without getting his approval. Sorreiro was not a very nice guy and he made life miserable for me for a while. Eventually he realized that I was doing a good job, and, in early 1934, when the

A parade in front of the Fox Theater, which Roy managed. *Arizona Historical Society.*

Fox began to show a profit after three years of losses, he became much more friendly.

However, when he was transferred to California a few months later, I was not a bit unhappy. His successor, Homer Gill, was an old-time theater man who had been in the business for many years. He was a delightful guy, and we became very good friends for the balance of his life.

Homer moved the Arizona headquarters to Phoenix. He knew my friend, Louie Mueller, who was running the Aguirre Apartments for his aunts, and worked out a deal to make an apartment available for him whenever he was in Tucson.

After Homer Gill had been in Arizona for about a year, he brought an old friend down with him from Phoenix. I'll not use his name for reasons that will be obvious when I tell what happened. He, too, was an old-timer in show business and had held some important jobs, such as head of the theater chain owned by RKO (Radio-Keith-Orpheum) that made his name well known across the country. He told Homer, who spoke highly of him, that he was on a vacation.

The day after they arrived in Tucson, we went to lunch at the Pioneer Hotel. Before we finished lunch, a bellboy told me someone wanted to speak with me in the lobby. It was Lee Omdotf, a long-time Tucsonan, who showed me the front page of the *Los Angeles Times*. On it, there was a picture of Homer Gill's friend, under the caption "Wanted for fraud." The newspaper article told about his absconding with a large sum of money from his last employer.

Naturally, I was shocked. Lee gave me that section of the *Times*, which I folded so the article was covered up. After lunch, we walked back to the Fox and I had a chance to get Homer alone so I could show him the article.

He broke out in a cold sweat. He had cashed his friend's check for $500 that morning. We decided that I should call the Tucson Police Department and alert them about having a wanted man in our town, but they said they couldn't do a thing based merely on the newspaper article. Homer wanted the guy picked up before he left town with his $500 and who could blame him? That was a large amount of money in those days. He urged the police to immediately query the L.A. police department and advise them that the culprit was in Tucson.

The day and evening dragged by, with Homer more antsy all the time. He was afraid his friend would hop on a bus and take off. Nothing happened that evening, and Homer, in the meantime, was buying the guy dinner and putting him up in his Tucson apartment. We teased Homer unmercifully about how he had to sleep between the guy's bed and the front door so he could be sure he'd be available when the police did eventually show up.

Early the next morning, the police arrived and took the guy in tow. He returned all but about twenty dollars to Homer, who was much relieved at having his friend arrested. We kidded him about being pleased that an old friend was arrested—did he feel that way about most of his old friends?

While I was at the Fox, I was a close friend of the University of Arizona's football coach, Tex Oliver. I was a football nut. I attended every football practice and got to know all the players. I told them that if they came to the Fox, I'd let them in with their girlfriends on a pass. Obviously, I was quite popular with the kids, many of whom have been life-long friends.

One of the strange things I can't account for to this day occurred the first week in 1934. Overnight, the Fox Theater had a profit that week and continued in the black for several months. The same thing happened in practically every other theater the Fox West Coast Company owned up and down the West Coast. It was the first sign that the Depression was ending and, although business conditions were not extremely good, they were certainly better than they had been for three or four years before 1934.

During the period after 1934, it was necessary to do a lot of promotions to get people to come to the theater. We would give a new automobile away about once a month. For three or four weeks prior to the drawing we would give raffle tickets to everybody who came to the theater, so they could participate in the car drawing. We also had quite a few merchants in town giving raffle tickets to their customers so that they would have to come to the Fox the night of the drawing in order to be eligible to win.

I remember buying three Chevrolet coupes from Frank O'Rielly of O'Rielly Chevrolet Company for $420 each. We gave those cars away once a month for the next three months.

We also had Bank Nights, at which we would give $100 away to the person whose name was drawn at the theater that night. Regular customers of the Fox had to register their names in a large book with their addresses and telephone numbers. They were also assigned a number, and a ticket with that number was put into a large drum from which tickets would be drawn on the stage on Bank Night, which was every Wednesday.

If the winning ticket holder was not present to win the $100, it would be added to the following week's drawing, and it was quite common for the amount of money to build up to $500, $600, or even $800 on occasion. This, of course, would attract a lot of attention because that was a great deal of money in those days.

An enterprising man by the name of Byron Kemp started an insurance program under which he would insure people against losing if they weren't at the theater when their name was drawn. The insurance tickets sold for fifty cents, and he was quite successful in getting a lot of people to buy them. He also agreed that if you were present and had insurance, he would double your money.

All of this activity created a lot of excitement, and Bank Night got to be such a big affair that people would not only fill the theater but also stand out on the sidewalk, where loudspeakers would carry the results of the drawings.

One of our biggest promotions was the North Stone Avenue Gold Rush. This was a celebration of the completion of the Stone Avenue subway under the Southern Pacific tracks. Stone had been closed to traffic for nearly a year, and the merchants along it were hurting. They readily agreed to put up their share of the $1,000 that was to be given away at the Fox on the night the subway was opened.

The month leading up to that night was a time of much advertising by the Fox and the merchants, who were distributing raffle tickets for the drawing. To claim their prizes, the winners had to hold a ticket to the Fox, as usual. The promotion created a lot of excitement. We knew the theater would be packed, so we rigged up a public address system covering not only the street in front of the Fox but also the several blocks on North Stone between Congress and the subway. This made it possible for those along Stone to hear what was going on on the stage of the Fox.

On the stage we had an all-star cast of dignitaries. I had gotten our Arizona congresswoman, Mrs. Isabelle Greenway, to participate in the drawings. She was being visited at the Arizona Inn, which she owned, by former vice president Charles Dawes, whom she brought along to appear on our stage. Their presence, plus that of the Tucson mayor and a few other important citizens, gave the event a very respectable status.

After the smaller prizes were drawn for and awarded to the winners, the big prize of $500 cash was drawn for. When the ticket number was announced, the winner was about two blocks north of Congress Street. Because the street was closed to traffic, he came running down the middle of Stone with his wife in one hand and a daughter in the other. I didn't see that because I was acting as emcee on the stage.

The event caused the Fox to have the biggest box office receipts in its history. I recall that Harold Steinfeld, who owned Steinfeld's Department Store, told me the next morning that the crowd in downtown the previous evening was the largest he had ever seen.

All these drawings were in violation of state gambling laws, but because business conditions were tough, the public officials recognized there was no harm being done. They knew that they were honest drawings, that the public enjoyed them, and that they gave the theaters an opportunity to increase their revenue. Eventually, the events were outlawed again, but not until the Depression had practically ended and we were preparing for World War II.

One of the other highlights of the Fox Theater was the Mickey Mouse Club, which took place every Saturday morning. Youngsters under twelve years old were admitted for ten cents and were registered as members of the Mickey Mouse Club, which was operated by a fine lady by the name of Mabel Weadock. She was called "Aunt Minnie" and was very popular with the members of the club.

Every Saturday morning, we would have special ceremonies on the stage, during which she and I would make various kinds of presentations to the children. The theater would be jammed.

Still, to this day, I have gray-haired women and men who remind me that they were members of the Mickey Mouse Club when I would get up on the stage of the old Fox Theater.

I HAD AN interesting and unforgettable experience while at the Fox. Nearly every week some young guys would sneak into the theater by not paying. One of their group would buy a ticket and then go to one of fire exits and open the door so that his buddies could get in. Our ushers were on the lookout for this maneuver and generally could handle the transgressors. However, there was one tough kid, a football player at Tucson High, who would try to beat up the usher if he tried to stop him.

One afternoon we caught this roughneck in the alleyway to the Fox off of Congress Street. The boy tried to run away from us, but I caught him and tackled him. He pulled a knife from his pocket and was trying to cut me, but luckily the police were close by and took him in tow to the station.

They called his father and told him about the incident and that there was to be a hearing before a superior court judge in his chamber because this kid had been in several other scrapes. The father came down to see me and begged me not to press charges because if I did, his son would be sent to the Ft. Grant reform school. He said his older boy had spent some time there and he hoped the younger one would be spared the same fate.

I was asked to come to Judge Fred Fickett's chambers for the hearing. When asked if I wanted to press charges against the boy, I replied that all I wanted was for him to stop harassing our ushers. I told the boy that I would let him in free with his girl once a week and would pay him to guard our fire exits on weekends but that he had to behave himself.

The judge asked the kid if he was willing to accept my offer. The boy broke into a big smile and thanked me. He promised to do a good job, and I can say that he did. One night he caught three kids trying to sneak in the back exit off of Stone Avenue and bloodied a couple of them, much to the delight of a couple of ushers who saw the encounter from the upper exit landing.

The boy straightened out and turned out to be good friend of mine. He became a plumbing contractor here and had a good life until his untimely death from cancer.

While I was at the Fox, one of the most enjoyable weeks I experienced was while Ted Lewis, the famous bandleader who popularized the famous expression "Is everybody happy?" was in Tucson with his musical organization. One of his famous numbers was "Me and My Shadow," which was always accompanied by a clever dancer who danced before a spotlight that projected his shadow on a screen dramatically and in slow motion.

A couple of weeks before Ted Lewis and his band reached Tucson, his advance man arrived and helped set up a promotional program. He also negotiated an arrangement with us whereby Lewis would receive a portion of the box office receipts. One issue we had not agreed on when the advance man called his boss was the matter of the amount to be charged for admission. Our ticket price was normally forty cents. His advance man wanted to charge seventy five, which I contended would keep many fans away.

After explaining to his boss my position, he told me that the man on the other end wanted to speak to me. The man asked if I had ever seen Ted Lewis. I told him I had and that he was one of my favorite performers but that I thought the admission prices should be fifty cents. He proceeded to tell me how great a show Ted Lewis put on, how popular he was, and so on, and so forth.

I finally asked him whom I was speaking to. He replied, "This is Ted Lewis." I'll never forget what a great salesman he was—he not only was sold on himself, but he sold me on Ted Lewis. We compromised and charged sixty cents.

His group arrived four or five days in advance of their appearance and rehearsed late one night after the movie. Lewis was a marvelous guy and we spent every night for a week together, visiting night spots and restaurants in Tucson. I had a wonderful time with him. His show attracted huge crowds and validated his opinion of his popularity.

At about that same time, a black performer named Step-N-Fetchit was being featured in quite a few movies as a comedian. He was always shown as lazy, which stereotyped him, of course, but his funny lines and great delivery made him a popular star. He visited Tucson as part of a promotion for one of his pictures and spent a lot of time around the Fox.

He was a very smart hombre and good company to visit night spots with. He was very talented and, one evening in a small night club, he spent about an hour at a piano, playing tunes he had written as part of a musical production about a small black town in Oklahoma that hit oil when someone drilled a well for water. His story about the whole town when it suddenly became very rich was hilarious.

One of the most interesting show business personalities I had the good fortune to have as a friend was Bryan Foy, known as "Brynie." He was a member of the famous theatrical family known as "Eddie Foy and the Seven Little Foys." The Irish father, Eddie, was a legend in the theater, going back to the 1880s. He had been a star dancer and comedian at the time when Tombstone was in its heyday and had played there.

I got acquainted with Brynie when he called me from his office in Hollywood to ask if I knew the parents of a young woman named June Robles who had just been returned to her family here after having been kidnapped and held for about two weeks. Brynie got my name from a mutual friend at one of the studios. When I told him that indeed I did know June's father, Fernando, he said he wanted to talk to him about booking her to appear in theaters for a few weeks. The kidnapping, not too long after the Lindbergh one, had been highly publicized throughout the nation. Brynie thought that June would be a good box office attraction and wanted to sign on as her manager and booking agent.

He came down on the train the next day, and I met him at the station. We immediately hit it off in great fashion and became friends for the many years that Brynie was around.

I arranged a meeting with Fernando Robles, who had been a lifelong friend of mine going back to grade school days and continuing while we attended the university. Other theater people had attempted to sign up the Robles family for a personal appearance tour, but wisely

Fernando's family decided that June should not become a theatrical act. So although Brynie's visit to Tucson was fruitless in its original intent, it did give us a chance to become friends.

Brynie was an important guy in Hollywood as a sometime agent but he was even better known as a producer. He produced the first "All Talking Picture, 'The Lights of Old New York.'" If Brynie did nothing else, he still remains the creator of Hollywood's and the world's first "All Talking Motion Picture."

I visited him many times in Hollywood and had some fascinating evenings with him and his friends. He knew everybody, and we had a lot of fun "doing Hollywood." I met some of his siblings who were involved in the studios. His brother, Eddie Foy Jr., was a popular and busy actor who appeared in many films as a dancer, comedian, and character actor. Brynie also had a couple of delightful sisters, whom I met.

In 1939, before I left the Fox Theater, I had become weary of the company's policy of featuring double bills every week, eliminating opportunities for the kinds of promotions I enjoyed.

Show business was an important part of my early life. For the first few years after leaving the Fox, I had regrets because I missed the nighttime activities. But I was really fortunate that I made the decision to become the manager of the Tucson Sunshine Climate Club, a community organization whose purpose was to promote Tucson nationwide as a winter resort and health center. I had an opportunity to become acquainted with many people all over southern Arizona, which gave me a good base for the real estate business I entered in 1946 after my wartime service in the army.

A Few Show Biz Footnotes

THEATRICAL PEOPLE FEEL that they belong to a large family, which includes all other people involved in the theater. If an actor or an agent found himself in Tucson with time on his hands, you could be sure he'd head for the nearest theater to see the movie or a show as a guest of the management. During my "show biz" days, this brought me in touch with many characters—mostly, though not always, interesting and good people.

One afternoon while I was running the Rialto, a man with a five-day growth of beard, wearing an old hat and a pair of Levis held up with a rope belt came to the door of my office and asked if he could use a desk in the office to write some letters. He said he had walked over from the train station across the street where he had just arrived from Mexico. He was waiting for an evening train to Los Angeles.

As he introduced himself, it began to sink in to me that John Barrymore, the great star of Broadway and motion pictures, was standing before me. He said he had been fishing down at Guaymas and looked like a bum because he was on a relaxing vacation.

During the three hours he spent in my office, I sneaked out and used the phone in the box office to tell a reporter friend of mine at the *Citizen*, Don Still, that Barrymore was in my office and that I thought he was worthy of an interview. Don soon arrived, and Barrymore graciously answered his questions. He gave him enough information to write a story that ran in the *Citizen* the next day. I remember one comment Barrymore made. When Don asked him if he drank much tequila in Mexico, he said, "Why should I drink tequila in Mexico when I can get benzine in the U.S.?"

In 1926, we signed a contract for the Rialto with Warner Brothers to run a block of their movies, one a week, on the basis of that company's receiving a percentage of the box office receipts. It was customary under such an arrangement for the film company to have an agent be at the theater to check the ticket sales.

Warner Brothers sent to Tucson none other than the elderly parents of Jack, Harry, and Sam Warner to check the Rialto's box office. I'm sure it was considered a vacation for Mr. and Mrs. Warner, who stayed at the Congress Hotel across the street from the Rialto so they could enjoy our warm winter weather. They were delightful people. There really wasn't much for them to do, but I enjoyed their friendly, almost-daily visits.

Whenever a traveling road show was booked for the Rialto, an advance man would arrive about three weeks ahead of it to plant publicity stories in the newspaper, work with the theater manager in having posters displayed all over town in store windows (in exchange for passes to the show) and on billboards, and give the manager material to be used in newspaper ads before the show hit town. Some of these advance press agents were colorful guys, full of all kinds of the stories you'd expect from traveling salesmen—which they were.

I remember one by the name of Dick Mitchell, who would come through with one show or another out of New York every year. He would sometimes also be the business manager of the show company.

Those shows always were reserved seat affairs whose tickets were "hard tickets," different from the ones used for the regular movies. The box office receipts for road shows usually were split so that 75 percent went to the show company and 25 percent to the theater.

Dick Mitchell could hold a handful of tickets next to his ear and, just by riffling through them with his thumb, accurately count what his share of the box office receipts was for the evening. He'd do it very quickly and never made a mistake, so far as I knew.

Another show business guy I well remember was an old vaudeville performer who brought his act to Tucson every year. A week before he would play the Rialto, he'd have a steel burial vault placed in our lobby, surrounded by posters stating that the Great Escape Artist, Raffles, would soon be playing the theater and would escape from the sealed burial vault on stage.

Raffles's real name was Howard Golden. He was a tall, handsome, white-haired man who always drove an expensive new car and had an attractive lady with him whom he would introduce as his wife. Each year he'd have a different "wife" and generally a new car. After I got to know him quite well, I remarked to him that I noticed the annual changes. "There's nothing wrong in changing wives or automobiles," he said to me, "so long as you keep trading up." I couldn't argue with him: he could sure pick pretty ladies and fancy cars.

After he retired, he would occasionally come through and look me up. The last time I saw him, he said he had been very sick—and he looked it. He said he needed to borrow $100 from me so he could get to an old actor's hospital in Alabama to see if they could cure his cancer. He said if he lived he'd pay me back, but if I didn't hear from him I'd know he had died. I had a card from him when he first arrived in Alabama but that was the end of a long friendship with a man who escaped from burial vaults while he lived but lies buried in one someplace in the deep South.

One of the most attractive personalities to visit the Rialto was Ginger Rogers, who came through as one of the vaudeville acts on the circuit out of Chicago the first month she was in show business. She had won a national Charleston contest in Chicago in 1926 and was teamed with a pair of redheaded Charleston dancers in an act that kicked off a lifelong career for her. She was only about sixteen and was accompanied by her mother, who watched her like a hawk. I was very impressed by the young dancer and asked her if she would like to go dancing with me at the Blue Moon dance hall on the edge of town. She could go, she said, if her mother went along. We went to the Blue Moon after her last performance and spent about an hour there.

The interesting thing about that evening was that the actor Lew Ayres, to whom she was later married, was playing a banjo in the orchestra at the Blue Moon that evening.

Many years later, when she came to Tucson to help boost the sale of war bonds, I was in charge of the programs in which she was to appear at various places around town. I met her at the railroad station and spent most of the day and evening with her. I told her about her first visit to Tucson when she was just a teenager. She was divorced from Ayres at that time but said they were still friendly and that she would tell him about the 1926 evening when he was playing at the Blue Moon.

I later ran into her two or three times in New York City night clubs. She was always quite friendly, although I'm sure she never knew my name.

Sports

Baseball Was Early Tucson's Only Major Sport

BASEBALL IN TUCSON was, by far, its number one sport from 1885 until the University of Arizona's football team began to develop a following right after World War I, when it was selected to represent the West in an important 1920 bowl game played in San Diego between Arizona and Center College of Kentucky.

In the later part of the last century, several local teams competed with each other, but when an out-of-town team came around, all the best hometown players would join together into an "all-star" team. Many times they would beat the visitors, even though former big-league players were often included on the visiting teams' rosters.

My father, Manny Drachman, was usually manager of the Tucson team, even when he was in his early twenties and the youngest player on the team. When I was a boy, I heard many stories about what a great player he had been. He also had one hell of a reputation as a fistfighter, which apparently was important because many of the games included fights, during or after the game. He was once offered a professional contract by Charles Comiskey, who, at that time, owned the St. Louis Browns, before he acquired the Chicago White Sox, and for whom their ballpark is named. Dad's mother knew that, in those days, big-league ballplayers were largely roughnecks and wouldn't allow him to sign with Comiskey.

Visiting teams from Globe, Phoenix, Bisbee, and Cananea, Mexico, regularly played here at the old Elysian Grove ballpark. The base-

66

ball season here lasted almost year-round and attracted professional players during the cold weather in the East and Midwest.

My dad told me that the catcher did not stand immediately in back of the batter back then. Because he didn't have a large catcher's glove, a breast protector, or even a mask, the catcher would stand behind the batter, about twenty or twenty-five feet away, and catch the ball on its first bounce. The umpire stood in back of the pitcher.

One day a visiting player told my father's team that masks for catchers were now made, and he let the team know where it could order one, which the team did. Soon the mask arrived, and the catcher could crouch directly behind the batter. A few weeks later, the visitor who had told them about the mask came back to town and was shocked to see that the catcher was wearing a flimsy screen fencing mask that might ward off a dueling sword but certainly not a baseball. The team's next order was carefully revised.

The Tucson Greys was the best team in town. It was made up of a mixture of Mexican-American and gringo players and managed by my father. Two other Drachmans, his brother, Mose, and his cousin, Herb, also played on the Greys. There were two or three other teams in town and seldom did a Sunday go by without a ball game at the Elysian Grove.

My dad was a baseball nut. My mother told me several times how, for Christmas when I was about a year and a half old, they had lined up several little toys and a baseball on the floor for me. My dad was very pleased when I bypassed all the toys and picked up the ball, as though baseball was suddenly important to me.

Well, from the time I went to the first grade, I could go to the games at the Grove, which was only a block from our home. I saw many games, sitting in the old grandstand and chasing after foul balls that went over it.

Around 1914, the first professional baseball league in the area, the Border League, was organized. It included Tucson, El Paso, Albuquerque, and Phoenix, and it played several games a week. I used to rush home from school and head for the Grove whenever a game was played. Unfortunately, the league was ahead of its time and soon expired because of lack of attendance.

As little kids, we played baseball in the middle of Main Street, which was wide and carried little traffic. Most of our players were Mexican-American, and we'd play by the hour. When I was about nine or ten, we organized a neighborhood team and played kid teams

Roy as a member of the Tucson High 1924 state championship baseball team.

from other nearby neighborhoods (most neighborhoods fielded teams then). I remember going to see one of the Catholic Brothers at Marist College, which was a few blocks away, to arrange a game with the team from that school. We played several games with them on the field in their walled-in yard. John and Joe King, sons of a well-known southern Arizona rancher, played on the Marist team and became lifelong friends of my brother Frank and me.

When I was going to the Safford School in the sixth and seventh grades, there were class teams, and baseball was the number one game there, too, although we did play soccer on the school playground during the lunch hour.

After we moved to the north side of town, on Fifth Street and Fifth Avenue, we were living near three other Drachman families. With Byron, Cowan, and Dick Drachman, we formed a Drachman team of kids between twelve and fourteen years of age. We had trouble finding a place to play our games but finally discovered Mulberry Park, which covered a city block on the southeast corner of North Stone and Speedway. The park had trees around its perimeter, but the major portion was covered only with small weeds. The land was flat as a pancake and we decided to create a baseball field on it.

We got a bunch of kids to help us and we scraped the field, built a pitchers' mound, and laid out the diamond. We promoted the lumber poles and the chicken wire needed to build a backstop, and made ourselves a good ballpark, though about a week later a big windstorm hit town and blew over the backstop. We rebuilt it—sturdier this time—and played at Mulberry Park for two or three years, until we went to high school and played on the Tucson High School field.

When I was a junior in 1923, I played shortstop on the high school team and was a second string pitcher. My brother Frank was our catcher and our cousin Byron played first base. León Carrillo was our pitcher, and his cousin Joaquín Carrillo was our right fielder. We won all our games until University Week, when we played Phoenix Union School in the finals and lost 6 to 5. In 1924 we again went to the finals during University Week against Phoenix and won the state championship. We had a pretty good team.

In one informal meeting against the University of Arizona Wildcats, we played a nine-inning tie game, which I pitched. The next year, as a freshman at the university I was one of the players on the squad. Intercollegiate rules then prohibited freshman from playing on the varsity teams. I wasn't quite good enough to make the team anyway, but could have played later if I had remained in school.

There were several semipro teams in Tucson, and I continued to play baseball on them for several years after quitting school and working at the theaters. After a couple of years, I was invited to play on the Southern Pacific Rails, which was the best team in town. We played every Sunday against either a local team such as the Elks or the Club Latino, as well against teams from Globe-Miami, Phoenix, Bisbee, Douglas, and Nogales and against military teams from camps at Fort Huachuca and even from Mexico.

The S.P. team was made up of Mexican-American players except for Joe Wagner, our second baseman, and me, our shortstop. Nearly all the players were guys we had grown up with and who were our good friends, such as Willie and Fito Aros, Conejo Preciado, and Teddy Sonoqui. Mike Robles managed the team and was a good hustler but was known to be a bit of a "coyote" at times. We suspected that he didn't always give us a fair cut of our share of the gate receipts.

A few years later I organized a semipro team with some of those same players and served as its manager. Our star pitcher was Johnny Kellner, the father of Alex Kellner, who played for several years in the big leagues, and was a twenty-game winner one of those years. Even his grandsons played professionally.

I quit playing when I was twenty-seven. The Arizona-Texas League was organized about that time. My father was president of the Tucson Cowboys and had a strong hand in organizing the league, whose members included Phoenix, Globe-Miami, Bisbee-Douglas, Albuquerque, El Paso, and Tucson. After my father's health forced him to retire as president of the team, Hi Corbett took over and ran it for many years. Games were played five times a week, generally at night because of the heat. The Tucson Cowboys were a Cincinnati farm team. Frank Lane, known later as "Trader Frank," was in charge of their farm teams and made many trips to Tucson. I knew him quite well.

A sizable number of Arizona-Texas players moved on to the big leagues. Monte Pearson, who was a star pitcher in the big show, played here, as did Babe Dahlgren, Tucson's first basemen who became famous as the player who succeeded Lou Gehrig.

The league continued until World War II, when travel was restricted and most of the players went into the military. The war caused nearly all the small minor leagues to fold up.

In an effort to keep baseball alive during the war, I called a meeting of the managers of the local amateur and semipro teams and proposed that we organize a city league made up of four local teams and one each from Davis-Monthan Field and Marana Field. They liked the idea, so the City League was formed, composed of the Elks, the American Legion team of young players, the Southern Pacific team, the Club Latino, and the two military teams. Those last two had several professional players, including Gene Mauch, who played on the Marana team before moving to the majors to manage several teams there.

Games were played at City Ball Park, six nights a week. The admission charge was twenty-five cents. Attendance started out slowly but soon built to the point that large crowds of fans showed up and made the league a success. We had two umpires, one of whom was Slim Williams, a black man who knew his baseball and had the respect of both players and managers.

Following the end of the war, the City League gave way to the Arizona-Texas League, which was revived and provided fans with Class-C baseball.

The major leagues continued to play during the war, although the quality of players was not what it had been, because many of the stars were in the service. In the spring it was common for one of the big-league teams to stop off in Tucson and play a practice game with the U of A Wildcats.

One time, Joe McCarthy, who later managed the Yankees for many years, brought his big-league Chicago Cubs here to play the Wildcats. Before the game started, he happened to spot Chili Francis, who was going to umpire the game, with his paraphernalia on. A local boy who became a professional player, though never in the big leagues, Chili Francis was a hard-drinking, scrappy guy who after his playing days became a city fireman and Tucson's best umpire for local games. "Is that guy Chili Francis?" McCarthy said. "He used to play for me once. He was an alcoholic and would drink *paint!*" Chili was really a nice guy after he laid off liquor.

I remember an earlier visit the Chicago Cubs paid to Tucson to play the Wildcats at what is now Hi Corbett Field on their way home from their spring-training camp on Catalina Island. This was about 1928 and Rogers Hornsby, the greatest right-handed hitter who ever lived, was playing second base and managing the Cubs. The Wildcat pitcher was Rod Luscomb, a player I had played against in San Diego when our high school team went there in my senior year.

Rod had a pretty good fastball, which apparently was to Hornsby's liking. The second time he came to bat he pointed to the right field fence and promptly hit a home run over it. The next time he came to bat he pointed to the left field fence and knocked another one out of the park in left field. I saw this happen, and I've never forgotten it. (Incidentally, Hornsby is the only hitter whose major-league batting average exceeded 400 three times. One year he hit 424!)

Prize Fights and Other Sports Events in Early Tucson

LOCAL PEOPLE DIDN'T have much available for entertainment and recreation besides movie theaters during the 1920s and 1930s. They had to depend on local dance halls, prizefight promoters, and sports events at the U of A or Tucson High.

A local restaurant owner, Louie Gherna, began promoting prize-fighters in a Mickey Mouse arena he concocted in the downtown area, west of Church Street and south of Congress Street. It seated about three or four hundred fans on bleachers and a few ringside benches. It was poorly lighted and had practically no ventilation, but it attracted pretty good crowds at the biweekly boxing matches.

Most of the boxers were local Mexican-American boys or young men between the ages of eighteen and thirty. Some were fairly good fighters who had been in the game for several years and who had fought on cards in other cities. Nearly every year, some local fighter would establish himself as a local champion in the lightweight or middleweight division. Gherna would import a fighter from Mexico, California, or Phoenix for a match against the latest Tucson sensation, an event that, with the aid of local sportswriters, would attract good crowds.

One local fighter, Mike Quihuis, a welterweight at 140 pounds, beat all the local scrappers and won a few fights in El Paso and a couple of Arizona towns. A young guy in Phoenix by the name of Marion West was building a reputation as Arizona's best welterweight, having beat up on every man he met in bouts around the state. Finally, Gherna was successful in booking West to come to Tucson to take on Quihuis for the title of Welterweight Champion of Arizona.

The fight generated a lot of excitement. The arena sold out at increased ticket prices. As usual, the fight card included five or six bouts, with the preliminary ones lasting four rounds to give boxing rookies opportunities to test their skills against other local boxers. The main event was generally ten rounds long, the limit established by the state boxing commission

Finally, the main event fighters entered the ring and put on their gloves, which were inspected by the trainer or second of each fighter to be sure that the opponent didn't have a rock or horseshoe in his glove. The first round saw each fighter sparring to feel out his opponent. In the second round, Marion West unleashed his powerful right, which had helped him establish a record of ten knockouts in eleven previous fights, and he caught Mike flush on the chin. Down he went and out he was. Marion West was the Arizona Welterweight Champion, without question.

This was around 1930. Soon afterward, a fight promoter from Los Angeles by the name of Joe Levy came to town. He and I had a mutual friend in L.A. who told him to look me up, which he did as soon as he arrived. He was a short, heavyset man of about fifty who had once been a fighter himself, then a fight manager and promoter both at the Olympic Auditorium in L.A. and at the Olympic Coliseum in Portland. He had good connections with all the Coast fighters and their managers.

He wanted to promote fights in Tucson, and he came to the conclusion that the only place that would serve as a venue for the kind of fights he wanted to present was the old armory on South Fifth Avenue. I helped him make arrangements for its use as a location for his bouts as well as for his fighters to train.

He had to get a city license to promote fights here, and, naturally, Louie Gherna opposed him. A few of us supported Levy, who prevailed and was granted permission to stage his bouts at the armory, which he did every other week. Nearly all the main events were between fighters imported from the Coast who had built up reputations as winners there.

Almost before I knew it, Joe Levy made me "secretary and treasurer," without pay, of his "fight club," which promoted fights and wrestling matches here for about eighteen months. I paid off the fighters and wrestlers for him. I enjoyed being around these rather strange people, especially the wrestlers, who would come to town together in the same car but act as if they were mortal enemies in the ring. Before their matches, they would plan their scenarios for the evening and decide who would be the winner.

One thing Joe Levy told me has stood me in good stead a few times: "A fool writes letters, and a smart guy saves them." On several occasions I've let off steam by writing a letter about something that really irked me, held it for a day or two, read it, then tore it up, because I realized that if the receiver saved it, I might be embarrassed by it later.

In an arena on South Stone Avenue, which had been the headquarters for the Tucson Federation of Labor a few years before, a favorite "villain" wrestler by the name of Dutch Mandel from West Texas, who weighed only about 150 pounds, wrestled many, many times. He was a great performer. Fans loved to boo him because he would invariably do something during his matches to get them riled up. He always entered the ring with a cigar butt in his mouth, which he promptly spit in the face of his opponent. Of course the crowd would go crazy, booing him for the whole match—but no one could beat him.

A certain waitress from a local restaurant always sat at ringside and rooted against Mandel. Once he was thrown on the floor right in front of her and held there for a few minutes by his opponent. She took off her high heel shoe and pounded his bare back so hard she brought blood. Dutch started yelling at the top of voice, and the other wrestler let him up. When he got to his feet he turned and began cursing the waitress, who jumped up and fled the scene, amid much laughter from the crowd.

The Labor Temple arena had a low ceiling with a set of trusses that supported the roof just a few feet above the ring. One time, when Dutch was wrestling a favorite Mexican-Indian wrestler who went by the name of Yaqui Joe, he climbed up on the ring post and into the rafters to get away from his opponent. Yaqui Joe followed him up into the rafters and took chase, covering almost all of the arena, much to the delight of the crowd below.

Obviously, wrestling matches were hippodrome entertainment affairs, and from what I see on television from time to time, they still are frame-ups that only fools take seriously but that seem to attract large crowds.

Black Athletes and Local Sports

THE UNIVERSITY OF Arizona had few, if any, black students, and certainly no black athletes on any of their sports teams for many years. In 1924, the new football coach at Tucson High School (THS) was Syl Paulis. Paulis had produced a team at Nogales High that beat all the other high schools in southern Arizona and tied the Phoenix Coyotes team for the state championship. Phoenix High, at that time, was one of the largest high schools in the nation, with over 5,000 students.

Paulis was the first coach to encourage blacks to come out for football at THS. and was instrumental in discovering and developing a great halfback by the name of Hazen Daniels. Daniels ran through and over tacklers to help the Tucson High Badgers win the southern Arizona championship. After two successful seasons at THS, he graduated but, because of racial bias on the part of the U of A athletic department, wasn't given an opportunity to play for the U of A.

This U of A policy also deprived other good black athletes of a chance to play for the Wildcats. It was a disgraceful attitude and time in the history of a great university. Furthermore, it deprived its teams of some great players.

One such outstanding black track and football star was Joe Batiste, who was one of that family's great athletes. He starred in football, although track was his best sport. He was a dash man, but his real specialty was the 110-yard high hurdles. He broke the national high school record for running those and held it for several years.

Tucson's sports fans were very proud of Joe Batiste. In 1939, we thought it appropriate for him to compete in national track events. One of the most prominent national events was the annual Drake Relays, held at Iowa's Drake University in the early summer. High school stars competed in the Junior Drake Relays while the college stars competed in the Senior.

The problem was finding the money to send Joe. Tucson High couldn't provide sufficient funds, and Joe's family couldn't afford the $200 for his expenses, so I took it upon myself to raise the necessary money at $5 here and $10 there. That wasn't easy to do in the later part of the depression, but we got the job done and paid for his round-trip railroad fare and expenses.

The favorite to win was a fine high hurdler at the college level named Walcott, who had won the high hurdle title in the National Intercollegiate Championship a few weeks before. Joe Batiste competed in the Junior high hurdle event and easily won it at fourteen seconds flat, the high school record. As a result, he was invited to compete in the senior high-hurdles competition and race against Walcott. Joe won that race, too, beating Walcott and all the other college stars.

The Amateur Athletic Union, the AAU, recruited a team of the winners at Drake and sent them off to Europe to compete in the summer of 1939. Joe Batiste was on that U.S. team and performed very well. However, Adolph Hitler decided to start World War II just at that time. Our American track team found itself in one of the nations that Hitler took over without a fight and, as I remember it, the American Embassy had to intervene and get exit visas for the members of the team to come home from the war zone, post haste.

Joe returned to Tucson as a hero and track star, but that didn't get him a scholarship at the University of Arizona. Fortunately for him, Arizona State was more aggressive about the advantages of opening their doors to black athletes and granted him a scholarship. He starred in both football and track for the two years he attended ASU before the ongoing war became a duty he readily accepted. Joe Batiste, as was true for many other young men and women in those times, never achieved his full potential, but there is no question that he was one of the greatest athletes ever produced in the Old Pueblo.

Joe had a younger brother, Fred, who was also a great athlete. Fred starred on the Tucson High Badger football team and was elected captain even though there were only two other blacks on the squad. That team, incidentally, was unbeaten and won the Arizona State Championship.

The pressure for blacks to be treated equally was building rapidly and, with the drafting of men of all colors into the armed services, the barriers against blacks competing on Wildcat teams at the U of A were soon lifted. As I recall, Fred Batiste entered the University and did very well as a halfback for the Wildcats. I believe he attended for a year before entering the armed services. He was very popular with the fans and his teammates.

The Batistes plowed some virgin ground in local and U of A athletic circles and it's a shame that more people don't know about their accomplishments. Since their pioneering days, hundreds of young black men and women have made their mark on Tucson and Arizona sports teams, but the Batistes opened the doors for them.

First Broadcast of a U of A Sports Event

SOON AFTER I entered Tucson High School in the fall of 1920, I established a friendship that led to what I believe was the first broadcast of a University of Arizona football game. At the time, the only communication by radio in Arizona was through individuals known as "hams," most of whom had built their own sets. There were no commercial radio stations yet.

Going to high school with me were quite a few veterans of World War I who had not finished their schooling before they went into the service. The federal government had set up a financial support program for them (something like the later GI Bill) called the "Board Students" program. This meant we had a substantial number of fellows in school who were several years older than most of us—which, if nothing else, made for a good football team.

One of those fellows was Kenneth Yeazel. He and I became good friends. He had been in communications in the army and knew a lot about a new gadget called "radio." I had never seen a radio and certainly never listened to one. Kenneth, my brother Frank, and I got to be good friends. One evening in 1922, Kenneth invited us to come out to his family's home in the suburbs to see what a radio looked like and to listen to some "programs," which were incredibly different from anything you hear today. His country home was located way out in the desert, on the northeast corner of Alvernon and Speedway, which, today, is right in the middle of the eastern part of Tucson.

His radio set, which he had built himself, was located in an outbuilding about the size of a one-car garage. We would go there in the evening and listen to whatever stations he could pull in from places as far away as Los Angeles and Denver, which had some powerful stations. Two of us would split a headset and each listen with one ear. There were no such things as speakers.

Some of the programs were quite interesting. There was a station on Catalina Island that would broadcast messages to, and receive them from, Los Angeles. We would listen in on those conversations, generally between a husband and a wife, with the husband explaining that he couldn't get back from Catalina when he had promised. Many times you could tell that the speakers had had a few too many, which provided us with some of radio's first comedy shows.

After a few weeks, because we were borrowing the family car for our trips, my father naturally asked my brother and me where we were going on so many evenings. We told him that we were going to visit a radio station, though it was really a private radio, a two-way communication. It was like a ham radio set that enabled the operator to talk to other people who had radios.

He said that he would like to go out with us. So he and his business partner, Ben Goldsmith, who was a nice, elderly gentleman, went along one evening. We got to Kenneth's considerably after dark because the signals came in best after ten o'clock.

When Ben Goldsmith put one of the earphones to his ear and listened to the conversation, he couldn't believe he wasn't listening to a telephone. In fact, he borrowed a flashlight, went outside, and walked all around the little shack, looking for a telephone line. He finally came back, shook his head, and said, "Well, I just can't believe that radio thing works—but I guess it does." My father likewise was excited, and he understood why we went out there so often to listen to this new gadget.

Before radio, Tucson had its way to keep up with sports. When the World Series was being played, the *Tucson Citizen,* located then on the northwest corner of South Stone and Jackson Street in a two-story building, would have a sports reporter with a megaphone lean out the second floor window and announce the play-by-play to the crowd gathered on Jackson Street as reports came over the wire. I well remember rushing down from class at the university in October of 1924 (the only year I attended college), to listen to reports of the Series between the New York Giants and the Washington Senators, the latter of which had the incomparable Walter Johnson pitching for them.

My father had been a sports fan all his life, and he especially loved baseball. During the World Series, played in the East at a time in the mornings when his theater, the Opera House, was not being used, he decided to have a Western Union station installed in the back of the stage to pick up the telegraphed play-by-play of the game. A Western Union telegraph operator would come over in the mornings and begin receiving the story of the game, via Morse code, which she would type up. Then my father would go on stage and read the play-by-play reports as they came in, usually a half inning at a time.

For visual effect, he had set up a large posterboard on the stage with a diamond painted on it and had rigged up an apparatus that would allow him to move a small baseball around the diamond as he "called" the game. He would open the theater and allow anyone to come in to listen to the game, free of charge. Of course, his arrangement also enabled *him* to hear the games first hand.

After he found out about the radio, he realized that it was something people in Tucson were becoming interested in. When he learned that there were several hundred radio sets in town, he decided that it would be great fun to actually broadcast one of the out-of-town University of Arizona football games.

I can't remember exactly what game he chose, but he did set up an arrangement whereby he could read accounts of the game over the radio as they were received through the Western Union wire in the basement of the Opera House.

I believe that was the first time a University of Arizona athletic contest was ever broadcast over the air. Many fans enjoyed it, and he received letters from quite a few, commenting on the fun they had listening to the game.

Kenneth Yeazel went to work for the police department soon after he finished school. He was put in charge of communications and built a radio set for the department. As the years went by and radio technology developed, Kenneth stayed with the job. I believe he spent his entire working life as a police officer in charge of radio operations. He played a major role in the development of a modern communication system for Tucson's police department.

Del Webb and the New York Yankees

DEL WEBB AND the Del E. Webb Construction Company were an important part of my life for thirty years. I became associated with the Webb Company in 1948, when they came to Tucson to construct 700 residential units in what later was known as Pueblo Gardens.

If there ever was such a thing as a self-made man, Del E. Webb certainly qualified, as did his partner, L. C. Jacobson, who grew up in Tucson but moved to Phoenix to work for Del and who later became Del's partner. Neither man ever attended a university, but both became millionaires.

The Del E. Webb Company was one of America's largest construction organizations. The company built veterans' hospitals, not only in the western states but also in many midwestern and eastern cities. It also built the two stadiums in Kansas City where the major-league baseball and the NFL football games are played and the stadium in Orange County where the California Angels have played for many years. During World War II, the Webb Company built thousands of residential units for the army, the navy, and the marines, as well as many other facilities at camps and bases throughout the nation, including Hawaii.

Del had been a semipro baseball pitcher in the Fresno, California, area. He earned a living by being a carpenter but never lost his ambition to be a big-league ballplayer. Although he didn't accomplish that, he did become an owner of one of the most important major-league teams.

In 1945, he, Dan Topping, and Larry McPhail acquired the New York Yankees organization, which included Yankee Stadium, from the Ruppert estate. Their timing was perfect. The steep inflation that immediately followed the war had not yet begun, so they bought the Yankees at a very good price.

Dan Topping was a member of a millionaire family that had gotten rich in mining tin and other metals overseas. He knew little about baseball and even less about big-time business.

Del Webb, on the other hand, was a highly organized businessman who ran his company "by the book." He established rules and regulations for his employees in almost every phase of the construction business.

Larry McPhail was a smart and experienced baseball executive. He also could be difficult to get along with; however, he added the kind of know-how this new team of baseball owners needed.

Not long after the trio bought the team, they recovered nearly all of their purchase price from the sale of the ballparks in Kansas City and Newark, which had been owned by the Ruppert estate when it sold the Yankees.

The trio was an unholy one, and, before long, personality clashes became an almost everyday problem. As a result, Webb and Topping bought out McPhail's interest in the club.

When Webb became involved in major-league baseball, it was more of a game than a business. Del changed that. I've been told by other big-league executives that he had a great deal of influence in the establishment of business principles not only by the American League, in which the Yankees played, but also in the operation of other major-league teams that followed his example.

Webb and Topping owned the Yankees during one of the two great periods in the history of that ball club. During the twenty years between 1945 and 1965, they won about twelve or fourteen pennants and several World Series. The Yankees, without doubt, was the most important sports franchise in the world.

However, in those days, the ball club did not make a great deal of money. I saw the annual profit-and-loss statements for several years, and usually the profits were in the range of a half million dollars, which, of course, is peanuts today. When Del and Topping sold the Yankees to CBS, they did indeed make a nice profit; however, the price was nothing compared to what such a franchise would bring today, especially when you consider that Yankee Stadium was part of the deal.

When Webb, Topping, and McPhail bought the Yankees in 1945 they paid $2.8 million. They acquired not only Yankee Stadium and the ballparks in Kansas City and Newark but also over 400 players, some 260 of whom were in the service. Webb and Topping bought out McPhail's interest in 1947 for $2 million. They sold out in 1965 for $17 million.

One of the most important moves Del made was the signing of Casey Stengel as manager of the Yankees. Casey had been a big-league player and was the manager of the Oakland, California, team when Del and Topping signed him on. Del happened to be in Tucson one evening and told me that after dinner, we had to go to the Southern Pacific Railroad Station to meet the train, because Casey Stengel was coming through on his way to report to New York as manager of the Yankees.

We met Casey and had a nice visit with him at the station during his fifteen- to twenty-minute stopover. I told him that I had been going to the World Series nearly every year, and he replied that if I wanted to see it for the next few years, I'd better plan to be in New York in October. How right he was! He won five consecutive pennants as manager of the Yankees. Fortunately for me, I saw every one of the World Series games during that five-year period.

The first World Series the Yankees won for Webb and Topping was in 1947, the same year the Brooklyn Dodgers won the National League pennant with Jackie Robinson, big league's first black player, as their second baseman. Excitement was at a fever pitch in New York City. Although the National League had begrudgingly accepted a black player, there was no certainty as to what the reaction would be by the Yankee players.

The idea of a "subway series" added to the aura of the games, and every seat was filled with a fan expecting fireworks. Jackie Robinson was one great athlete and it was quickly apparent that he belonged where he was, that he had the ability to be a true big leaguer. Early in the game, he reached first base and began his psychological antics to upset the pitcher by threats on every pitch to steal second base. Then he finally broke for second. The call was close, but Robinson succeeded in taking Phil Rizzuto out of the play by hitting him hard and knocking him down. He was safe, and when Rizzuto jumped up the crowd roared, expecting him to charge Jackie and perhaps have a fight. There was electricity in the air—but only glares were exchanged as far as the crowd could tell. Jackie had made his point: he was not backing off one bit in playing the game as hard as he could.

I believe every fan learned respect for him as a player and as a man on that play. He played well throughout the Series, proving he could both field and hit as a big leaguer.

DURING THOSE HEYDAYS of the New York Yankees, a contingent of Arizona baseball fans and friends of Del would go to the Series every year.

In order to properly entertain his guests from Arizona, Del had a special room set up on the lower level of Yankee Stadium, which was known as the Arizona Room and which was decorated with color photos of the state. On game day, we would gather there around eleven in the morning, have a couple of drinks, help ourselves to a magnificent spread for lunch, and then go to our box seats to watch the game. After the game, we would again gather in the Arizona Room, have a little libation, and wait for the crowd to disperse so that we could get in our limos for the ride back to our hotel. Eventually, an invitation to the Arizona Room during the Series became coveted by politicians, sportswriters, and celebrities from around the country.

But the real highlight of any Series the Yankees won was the victory dinner party. Those were relatively small, and I was fortunate to be invited to two of them. They were held at the Waldorf Astoria Hotel, the official headquarters for the Yankees during the Series.

Of course, all the Yankee players, as well as officials and their staff, were there. In addition, one or two stars of the entertainment world who happened to be appearing in New York at the time were also invited and performed at the dinner. There was always a dance band, so dancing was one of the evening's activities.

Sofie Tucker, a worldwide favorite, put on a memorable performance, after which she danced with Casey Stengel, much to the delight of everyone. Spending such an evening with famous ballplayers and the special guests was indeed a supreme treat for any baseball fan.

We were living "high on the hog" in those years and enjoying every minute of it—except for one game. That was the seventh game of the 1948 World Series, when the hated "bums" from Brooklyn beat the Yankees. We were sick at heart but had to accept the fact that our Yankees had just won more than their share of Series games.

The Brooklyn Dodgers in those days were many notches below the Yankees. Their ball teams were nearly as good, and sometimes better, but the class ended there. I well remember the men's bathroom on the mezzanine in old Ebbetts Field. There were thirty-two urinals by actual count, and only *one* wash basin. Need I expand?

Of course, not everyone was upset as we were. On the way back to our hotel after that infamous game, we had to drive through Harlem. On several corners, celebrating black Dodger fans were offering those in limos, who they were certain were Yankee fans, black armbands to observe our mourning over the Yankees' loss to the Dodgers. They were delirious that Jackie Robinson and his teammates had won the Series.

Del was certainly one of the most powerful owners in the American League, a fact I saw firsthand proof of. I was with two or three executives of the Webb Company at the Beverly Hilton Hotel in Los Angeles when he got a long-distance call. We all could hear the conversation.

Del said, "Well, that does it. That bastard has got to go. He's through."

After he hung up, he told us that Happy Chandler, commissioner of baseball at the time, had canceled the deal between the Yankees and the Detroit Tigers for a trade that would have brought star first baseman Dick Wakefield to the Yankees.

About ten days later, it was big news on the sports pages that Happy Chandler had indeed been fired as Commissioner of Baseball. Del was true to his word.

On July 4, 1974, Del died, and, unfortunately, most of those who used to attend the World Series in the Yankees' glory years are no longer around either. Del left a sizable fortune, which was used to create the Del E. Webb Foundation. That foundation has been generous to both the University of Arizona and Arizona State University, as well as to other charitable organizations in Arizona and California.

Great World Series Trips and Athletes

BY THE TIME I was about six or seven years old, I had been taught by my father to read the scores of major-league baseball games in the Tucson daily papers. For some reason, I adopted the New York Giants as my favorite team and followed them closely. They won more than their share of games and, every year or so, would play in the World Series.

When I was a kid, I played baseball, as did nearly all boys. As I got older, I began to follow local teams and players. My dad managed a team off and on, and I was bitten severely by the baseball bug. I played on the Tucson High team in my junior and senior years and we won the state championship in 1924.

Tucsonans in the infantry at Camp Roberts, California, in 1944. *Left to right* Privates Roy Drachman, Carlos Calles, James Young, Gilbert Ronstadt (Linda's father), Carl "Butch" Clark, Dick Drachman, and Corporal Gladney Stitt. *Photo by Ben D. Gross.*

I wanted badly to be a big-league ballplayer. I had everything needed except that I was slow, too small, didn't have a strong arm, and couldn't hit—otherwise, I was a great prospect! However, those minor faults didn't keep me from loving the game and becoming involved with other fans in promoting professional baseball through my part in Tucson's entry into the Arizona-Texas League.

Hi Corbett, twenty years older than me and a kindred soul regarding baseball, was president of the Tucson Cowboys and leader of us baseball nuts. Neither he nor I had ever seen an official big-league game but swore we would some day.

In the summer of 1944, while I was in the service at Camp Roberts, I met Hi in Los Angeles to see a ball game between the big-league all-stars who were in the military on the West Coast, and the stars of the Pacific Coast League. We made a pact that when the war was over we would go to the World Series.

When the war ended in the summer of 1945, we began planning our trip to see the World Series that fall. Detroit won the American League pennant, and the Chicago Cubs won the National League. That year, by the way, was the last time the Cubs played in the World Series.

The Series started in Detroit and because of the continuing war-time travel restrictions, the teams would make only one trip between games. Three were to be played in Detroit, followed by a travel day for the train trip to Chicago.

We invited Jack Martin, a native Tucsonan and an old friend, to join us in our trip to the Series. It turned out that he was a close friend of a man by the name of Dick Muckerman, who was owner of the St. Louis Browns. The Browns had won the American League pennant the year before. He and Jack were both in the ice business and had joint deals supplying ice for refrigerated fruit and vegetable

Left to right Stanford and, later, pro quarterback Frankie Albert, with Roy and Hi Corbett, about 1950. *Ray Manley photo.*

railroad cars. Muckerman was a nice guy, with plenty of money, and traveled in his own private railroad car with room for his entourage. His group included his wife and daughter, his attorney—who thought it necessary to carry a gun—and his tall, attractive secretary, about whom there were rumors of a romance with her boss.

Anyway, it was an interesting group, and we were soon much involved with them, as well as with some other friends of Muckerman's from St. Louis. Dick kept an ice chest in his suite, and liquor flowed freely. Hi and I were thoroughly enjoying the big-city World Series experience. Muckerman got us good seats and the games were exciting. Hank Greenberg was the principal Detroit star, although "Prince" Hal Newcomb carried a lot of weight as one of baseball's premier pitchers.

We traveled in Muckerman's private railroad car after the three Detroit games. Hotel rooms in Chicago were impossible to get, but I had called in advance and asked my friend Ernie Byfield, who owned the Sherman House, the Ambassador East, and the Ambassador West Hotels, to reserve us a two-bedroom suite, which he promised to do. Fortunately, he forgot, and instead invited us to stay in his palatial suite at the Ambassador East, so we didn't suffer. Incidentally, that was the first time I saw television; I didn't think it was very good.

At the end of six games each team had won three, and a seventh game was necessary, which put us fans who were seeing our first Series in hog heaven.

The Sunday before the last game was bitter cold. Cards and sightseeing trips were our choices for ways to spend the day, but an old friend of mine, Irving Phillips, had other plans for us. Irving had gone to high school in Tucson and had worked with me as an usher at the Opera House. By '45 he had been a banker in Chicago for many years and enjoyed a fair degree of success. He never married, and he knew every nightclub in town. He showed us the town when Chicago was really quite a town, especially at night.

Despite the cold, he insisted that we go to see the Chicago Bears play a football game against the Pittsburgh Steelers at Comiskey Field. It was too cold for baseball, he said, but just right for football.

Irving had been born without an arm below his right elbow. He was a huge man, about six feet five and around 300 pounds. He wore a large overcoat and looked like Man Mountain Dean, the famous wrestler.

When we came out of the game, there were no cabs in sight and the streetcars had people hanging all over them, so there was no chance to get on one of them. Irving told us to follow him to a nearby side street where there was little traffic. He stepped out into the middle of the street and stopped a car with a middle-aged couple out for a Sunday drive.

He told the driver we were detectives. He showed them the inside of his overcoat label, as though it were a badge, so fast no one could see it. He said we had to get to the police station downtown, which happened to be across from our hotel, in a big hurry. The couple were pretty gullible and told us to pile in. I was scared to death we'd all end up in the hoosegow.

The next day my traveling companions and I went to the ball game at Wrigley Field. We got there very early, as we liked to watch the teams work out. We had box seats on the first base side of the stands—very good seats about fifty feet back from the field. Before I sat down I heard someone shouting my name: "Roy! Roy!" I finally spotted where the shouts were coming from. Irving Phillips was on the field calling for me to come down.

I worked my way through the crowd to the gate leading to the field. An usher stopped me, but Irving, big as a mountain, told the usher to open the gate. Here I was, then, on Wrigley Field before the seventh game of the World Series along with a few worthy dignitaries. Irving introduced me to Arch Ward, sports editor of the *Chicago Tribune,* one of the most important sportswriters in the country, who, by the way, came up with the idea for both the annual all-star baseball game and the all-star football game.

The two starting pitchers, Hank Borowy for the Cubs and Hal Newhouser for the Tigers, were in the middle of warming up. That didn't stop Irving from taking me over to them and interrupting their throwing to have them shake hands with me about ten minutes before the game was to start.

While I felt pretty queasy being where I had no business, I was in a baseball fan's heaven, right in the center of such an important event, with 45,000 people looking on. The Detroit Tigers won the game and the Series, and the Cubs have never recovered, although it's been over half a century. They were jinxed in '45 and still are!

HI CORBETT AND I thoroughly enjoyed that first World Series in 1945, and we resolved to see many more. However, in 1946 the two St. Louis teams, the Cardinals and the Browns, won the two major-league pennant races and played all the Series games in St. Louis. That didn't excite baseball fans, particularly Hi and me, so we decided not to go to the Series that year.

The next season we did go. The Yankees, under Webb and Topping, with the able professional leadership of George Weiss, had put together a winning combination that won the 1947 American League pennant and played the Brooklyn Dodgers, as I recount earlier in the book. New York City proved to be a paradise for a couple of guys on the loose that year, and we swore we'd go to the Series again the following year, 1948. But New York wasn't to be the venue. That year the Cleveland Indians, who had trained in Tucson for two years, won the American League pennant and played the Boston Braves, with the first game scheduled for Boston.

Bill Veeck, principal owner of the Indians, was my good friend. I had met Bill's father, who was president of the Los Angeles Angels, when I was about twenty years old. My dad knew Mr. Veeck through Dad's connections with baseball in Tucson. Bill lived in Tucson after World War II, before he bought the Indians. I used to visit him at his ranch out east of town near where the Rocking K Ranch is, and, once in a while, he would have lunch with me in town.

A couple of years after the war, Bill bought the Indians and successfully operated the club for several years. He later sold that team, and, several years after that, acquired the Chicago White Sox, which he built into a pennant winner.

Bill took good care of Hi and me during that '48 Series, even arranging for us to ride on the special train taking the Indians back to Cleveland after the first two games in Boston. In the stateroom right next to us were Abbott and Costello, who also sat next to us at all the games. They added to the fun no end.

When we arrived in Cleveland the next morning, some 10,000 fans were at the station, and as we ran through the crowd along with the players people patted us all on the back, believing we were part of the squad. It was exciting.

Bill Veeck knew how to entertain the press: he realized that was the key to his success. For the whole three days that the teams and the sportswriters were in Cleveland, he threw an endless party at one of the hotels. It was some bash!

The Indians won three of the first five games and had to return to Boston for another game. Again, we traveled on the train with them.

We were met by a Boston cabdriver with whom we had gotten acquainted the week before. He had by chance picked us up as we came out of the first game and showed us Boston that afternoon. We invited him to come to our suite for a drink, and because we had an extra ticket for him, he took us to the game the next day. After that second game he drove us to the station and said that if we came back for another game in Boston, he would be our chauffeur. He also promised to drive us the next year if Boston was in the Series.

Well, the next year, the Yankees won and we traveled to New York. I had written Stanley, our Boston driver, and told him we'd miss him. On the morning of the first game in New York, we were in our hotel getting ready to go down and get a cab to the game when the phone rang. It was Stanley. He was in the lobby of our hotel ready to take us to the game. He had driven his cab down that morning from Boston to keep his promise to take us to the World Series! We were thoroughly convinced that when a Boston cabdriver commits to picking you up, he really means it.

ANOTHER UNUSUAL WORLD Series story occurred in 1950, when the Yankees played the Whiz Kids from Philadelphia. The Yankees won the first two games in New York and then had to go down to the City of Brotherly Love for the next two. A special train was put together, which included cars for the Yankees, the sportswriters, and a car full of us Yankee rooters from Arizona, who always attended the World Series when the Yanks were in them. The Yankees had even arranged for musicians and a magician to be in our car to entertain us.

I had gotten tickets for about a dozen fans from Tucson through my connections with Del Webb, At first the wives didn't want to go to Philadelphia, but, at the last minute changed their minds. Hi Corbett and I gave up our tickets because Hi had been told he could pick up four tickets in Philadelphia before the game from a produce man he knew from Phoenix. The train was arriving in plenty of time to allow us to go to the produce house for the tickets.

The train stopped at the North Street Station, where busses were to take the players and fans to Shibe Field for lunch and the game. Hi and I remained on the train, because the downtown station was near the produce district. We had the whole train to ourselves for the short ride downtown.

We went out to get a cab, but there was a line a mile long. We were told to go to a nearby hotel where we might have better luck. There, too, a large crowd was waiting for taxis. We tried bribing the cab starter with no success. We walked to other hotels but struck out. Time was wasting. It was about noon, and the game started at one. We found ourselves in a ridiculous situation. Here we had traveled 2,500 miles, had gotten tickets for a dozen people, and now we were five miles from the ballpark with no tickets!

We were getting desperate, walking around downtown Philadelphia and completely helpless. Finally, we were standing on a busy corner when a pickup truck with a young man driving it stopped for a red light. Hi said, "Follow me." He opened the door to the truck and we both piled in, much to the surprise of the driver. Hi said, "Young man, you're going to take us to the ball game, but first we have to go pick up our tickets at a produce office."

The kid was in shock. He said he was working and couldn't do it without talking to his boss. So he called him at a nearby phone, and the boss said OK, as long as we took him with us. We picked up his boss, who rode in the back of the truck, went by for the tickets, and got to the ballpark just as they were playing the national anthem. It was a close call. We saw the game and joined the party at a downtown hotel for a feast before boarding the private train for the big city. The Yankees did things in style, and we enjoyed every minute of it.

I could go on for pages reciting exciting and humorous incidents connected with the more than ninety World Series games I've had the pleasure of seeing in New York, Los Angeles, Oakland, Brooklyn, Baltimore, Pittsburgh, and Philadelphia, but I think I've told enough yarns to show how much fun I've had from baseball.

I ALSO HAD the pleasure of meeting many of the owners of big-league teams, sportswriters such as Grantland Rice, Damon Runyon, Westbrook Pegler, Gordon Cobbledick, Braven Dyer, Ring Lardner Sr., and too many others to mention. I saw the famous home run that the Giants outfielder, Bobby Thompson, hit to win the pennant for his team in the last game of the season against the Dodgers, as well as Don Larsen pitch the perfect no-hit, no-run game against Brooklyn in the World Series.

I was once asked if I had known many big-league baseball players. Through having had the Cleveland Indians train in Tucson for forty-seven years, I met and knew many, many famous players and managers. The list is too long to name them all, but a few include Ty Cobb, Rogers Hornsby, Lou Boudreau, Joe "Flash" Gordon, Tris Speaker—who was one of the nicest—Al Simmons, former Wildcat Hank Leiber, Al Schack, Bob Feller, Bob Lemon, Satchel Paige, Yogi Berra, Al Lopez, Billie Martin, Dizzy Dean, Bill McKecknie, the only baseball manager to become a 33d Degree Mason, and many others.

Another player I knew well, because he lived in Tucson for several years, was Hal Chase, "Prince" Hal, said by old-timers to be the greatest first baseman who ever played the game. Even before the "Black Sox" game-fixing episode in the 1919 World Series, Hal Chase was accused of fixing ball games in cahoots with gamblers, and he was booted out of baseball for life. For some reason he ended up in Tucson and, knowing I was a rabid baseball fan, found his way to my office at the Opera House back during the Depression. He was a pitiful character, dressed in worn-out clothes, but still with the bearing of an elderly athlete. He had nothing—not even money for food—and I staked him many times to a square meal. He had two sons who lived up in the San Francisco Bay area and they would send a few bucks once in a while. As I remember, they were attending Santa Clara College and couldn't help him much. He would receive his mail from them and others at the Opera House. He finally disappeared—I don't know what happened to him. He was a perfect example of a talented man gone wrong for a few quick dollars.

Bill Veeck and the St. Louis Browns

I HAD SOMETHING to do with Bill Veeck's acquisition of the St. Louis Browns baseball team in the early '50s, which he gave an account of in one of the books he authored.

Del Webb and I were in St Louis on some business; he, to attend the dedication of a veterans' hospital that his company had built, and I to do more work on a large urban renewal project in which the Webb Company was planning to be involved.

The night before the dedication of the hospital, Del and I went to see a ball game as the guests of Fred Saigh, owner of the St. Louis Cardinals. We sat with him in his box. He and Del, who was co-owner of the New York Yankees at the time, spent most of the evening talking baseball.

After the game, as we were driving back to our hotel, Del jokingly

Roy and his friend Bill Veeck at a 1948 party to which all the guests brought a necktie for Veeck, who was famous for not wearing one. *Conchita and Sam Levitz photo.*

said that if Hi Corbett and I wanted to own a big-league baseball team, we could buy the St. Louis Browns—the present owners, Bill and Charles DeWitt, both of whom I knew, were in a bad financial bind and were about to lose the team to a note holder they owed a sizable amount of money to. At that time Hi, I, and two other men owned the Tucson Cowboys in the Class-C Arizona-Texas League.

Upon my return to Tucson, I called Bill Veeck, who, at that time, had sold the Cleveland Indians and was relaxing at his ranch at the foot of the Rincon Mountains, east of Tucson. I suggested that he come in and have lunch with me. He did, and I passed on the information Del had given me about the Browns. He said that he was interested in what I'd told him and would think about it.

The next morning he came to my office and said he'd like to use one of my salesmen's offices and a telephone, because his phone at the ranch was a party line. For the next two or three days he was constantly on the phone.

When I got home a day or two later, at about five in the afternoon, my housekeeper told me that Mr. Veeck had called and said he was going to pick me up and that we were going to drive to San Diego that night. He had learned that the man who held the note from the DeWitts was staying at the Del Coronado Hotel there.

We got there in time to have breakfast with this man, who said he would make a couple of phone calls and asked us to come to the Del Mar Race Track after we got a few hours' sleep.

When we arrived at Del Mar, we went to the club section where Bill's friend said he'd be. Bill was famous for never wearing a necktie, and I believe I'm one of the few persons who ever saw him with one on. The gatekeeper of the clubhouse said that Bill couldn't come in unless he a wore a tie, which they were glad to lend him. He had it on for perhaps one minute, or even less, as we entered the clubhouse section.

Bill worked out things and became owner of the St. Louis Browns, which was usually a pretty poor ball team, finishing last in the standings on many occasions. However, during the war years they had won the American League pennant and had played in the World Series against the St. Louis Cardinals. When the war ended and the many players who had been in the service returned to their teams, the Browns resumed their role as doormats for most of the other teams.

One of the things Bill did was to accept my suggestion that the Browns should move their spring-training program from Florida to Arizona. I told him that actually the best climate in the early spring for baseball was probably in Yuma and that he should consider it as a site for the Browns to train.

He agreed to consider it and have one of his executives, Rudy Schaffer, take a look at it. So I called a prominent man and a good friend in Yuma and told him there was a good chance that the Browns would come to Yuma to train if the ballpark, the dressing rooms, and other facilities were adequate. Naturally, he was excited and assured me that the needed improvements would be made. The Browns trained there for two years, until Veeck was more or less forced to sell the team to a group that ended up moving the Browns to Baltimore.

During the time that Bill owned the Browns, I spent a long weekend over the Memorial Day holiday with him and his wife, Mary Frances. It was a weekend I'll never forget.

Dizzy Dean was broadcasting the Browns' games then and was much in evidence. Bill organized a special Fans Day to honor Dizzy. One of the things he did was to present Dizzy with a letter signed by thousands of his fans. The signature collecting had been going on for several weeks, and the letter had thousands of names on it. Bill had the mayor present the letter, which was on a roller at the home plate, like a scroll. When the roller with the letter was unwound, it extended through the pitcher's box, into the outfield, and over the center field wall. Of course, the newspapers and electronic media covered the event. It was a typical Veeck promotion.

On Saturday night, Bill invited me to join him, Mary Frances, and

Harry Jones, one of the baseball writers from the Cleveland Indians, who were in town for a series of games, to have dinner with them at the roof garden of the Chase Hotel, where I was staying and which was the "in" place in St. Louis at the time. Frankie Lane, at his peak then, was the featured performer at the nightclub. A friend of the Veecks, he spent a considerable amount of time at our table.

After dinner, Bill ordered a round of Cherry Herring, a pleasant drink, for each of us. But instead of one glass of the liquor being served to each of us, he had four small glasses of it placed before each of us. Because that drink contains a small amount of alcohol, it's fairly harmless. After thirty or forty minutes Bill ordered another round of four drinks for each of us. We were feeling no pain and were enjoying the floor show starring our new friend, Frankie Lane.

After we finished the second round of Cherry Herring, another order of four drinks for each of us arrived. Bill was dancing with Mary Frances at the time. When he returned to the table he saw the drinks and asked the waiter who had ordered them, since he hadn't. The waiter pointed to a man at a nearby table whom Bill had been visiting with during the evening.

Bill wasn't happy with this man's generosity. He ordered the waiter to bring each of the four people at that table four rounds of whatever they were drinking. They weren't drinking after-dinner drinks, but were having either Scotch or bourbon cocktails. The sixteen sizable cocktails just about covered the table. It turned out that the guy who bought us the drinks was the manager of a hotel in Kansas City and was trying to romance Bill into the idea that if and when Kansas City had a big-league team, the Browns should stay with him at his hotel.

In a few minutes, a punch bowl appeared at our table, into which the waiter emptied a full bottle of Cherry Herring and placed a dipper in it.

Bill considered this a challenge. He whispered something to the waiter, who soon appeared with a dolly on which were four cases of the booze the people at the other table were drinking. Of course, everyone nearby saw what was happening and heartily laughed at the goings-on. Needless to say, that was the end of the "contest." Bill's antagonist waved a white flag of surrender with a napkin.

That was the kind of guy Bill Veeck was. He lived the good life and enjoyed people—important or unimportant, it made no difference to him.

After he got out of active involvement in baseball, he and Mary

Frances moved to Chicago, where I visited him several times. The last time I was with him he invited me to have lunch with him and go to a Cubs ball game at Wrigley Field.

We ate at a small hamburger joint near the right field gate to the bleachers. We sat outside in the backyard at a round table where several rough-looking fans joined us. Later, I asked him if he knew them. He said that he had seen them before and that they were "unknown friends." After lunch we went to the ballpark and sat in the bleachers with a lot of other "friends" of unknown origin. Bill did this every day the Cubs were in town. He could have readily gotten box or grandstand seats, but he preferred to be with his gang of common folks in the bleachers. That was Bill Veeck.

He died a short time after that. He's remembered by his thousands of friends and a wonderful family.

Golf Courses in Early Tucson

TODAY IN TUCSON, there are at least twenty-five to thirty golf courses, but it was not so long ago that there was only one. Then there were two, then there were three, and that was it for many years.

The first golf course I ever heard about in town was at the northwest corner of Campbell Avenue and Speedway. It was a nine-hole one and existed there for a number of years.

The first course I personally had experience with was at the Tucson Country Club, which was located at the southwest corner of Broadway and Country Club Road. The road on the east side of the course, Country Club, was named after it. It was a dirt, or "skinned," course as they called it in those days.

The fairways were scraped out of the desert, and the greens, which were about sixty feet in diameter, were made of fine sand soaked with oil. They were black, with a hole right in the middle, and were coated with a fine sand the golfer had to sweep from the ball to the hole with a special type of sweeper. This sweeper, mounted on a mop handle, was a piece of wood about eighteen inches long and three or four inches thick with carpeting wrapped around it. One of the player's necessary skills was the ability to sweep the sand so that it was smooth and even, without any large deposits of sand to slow the ball down. The secret, they used to say, was in the drag.

Generally a forty- to fifty-foot apron area surrounded the green.

There were practically no traps around the greens, although there were some along the fairway.

The tees were essentially large boxes of dirt, held in by two-by-six boards. They usually were six or so feet deep and ten to twelve feet wide. Beside every tee was a tin box about forty inches high, divided into two sections. One section contained sand, the other water.

The player would throw a handful of water into the sandbox, take up a bit of wet sand, and fashion it into his tee. Some fancier players had little rubber tees they would place the ball on top of. The normal golf tees, as we know them today, were available, but the ground was so hard you couldn't possibly use one.

The old Tucson Country Club had a very nice clubhouse that stood for many years after the golf course had been converted to a residential subdivision. The course was established in the early 1900s and lasted until about the 1940s.

In the early 1920s, the Tucson Municipal Golf Course was built in Randolph Park (known by some as Reid Park), which is where the north course is located today. This course was also a skinned one with the same type of tees, fairways, and greens as those found at the Tucson Country Club.

That is where I first played golf and thought nothing of the fact that the course was dirt, hard on balls, hard on clubs, and hard on the players. When dust storms came through, it was practically impossible to see or play, but we did anyway.

The first grass golf course in Tucson was at the El Rio Club, on the north side of West Speedway, just west of the Arizona School for the Deaf and the Blind. The El Rio Country Club was established by Hi Corbett, George Stonecypher, Don Fogg, and a man named Doug Leech, a Canadian who used to winter in Tucson.

They built the course and a small clubhouse as a real estate development. They hoped to sell homesites around the golf course, but it was located on the "wrong side" of the Southern Pacific tracks, and most people didn't want to buy there. In fact, not even any of the builders of the country club bought lots or built homes there. As a real estate development, it was unsuccessful.

However, as a golf course, it was popular because it provided Tucson golfers with an opportunity to play on grass. Many of the members of the Tucson Country Club, including myself, resigned and joined El Rio. It opened in 1929, just before the Depression started.

A lot of members had to drop their membership in El Rio during the Depression years, which imposed a great financial burden on the promoters of the course, who held on to their property by paying many of the bills themselves.

Eventually, as economic conditions began to improve in the community, many members came back to El Rio. For a good number of years, the members had wonderful times there. I well remember that we would have a golf choose-up every Sunday morning, when forty to sixty golfers would show up to play on the various teams.

During the tough days of the Depression, we used to play "ten cent Nassau," a game that usually has four points in it so that if you did not play well and lost, you would only lose a total of forty cents. Caddy fees were twenty-five cents for eighteen holes. Today, the caddy fees are around twenty-five dollars for eighteen holes—if you can find a caddy.

El Rio was the principal golf course for most players in Tucson until 1948, when the present Tucson Country Club was developed by a group of businessmen and golfers.

Those promoting the Tucson Country Club included Harold Steinfeld, Andrew Pizzini, Monte Mansfeld, George Amos, Oliver Drachman, Ted Shoenhair, and one or two others.

The initiation fee was $5,000, which the hundred charter members each paid. They were also given a chance to draw a lot at the same location around the golf course, which they could buy by applying part of the initiation fee and the rest in cash.

An excellent golf course was created, southeast of the confluence of Tanque Verde Creek and Pantano Wash. The buildings that had been part of the McDonald Farm, which had been owned by a woman and her son, were converted to a clubhouse and to other buildings needed by the country club.

That area is still a fine residential one. The golf course has been one of the most popular ones in the Tucson area.

After that course was built in 1948, another wasn't built for several years.

Then the Oro Valley course came along, followed soon after by the Forty-Niner's Club and others. Tucson had become a mecca for golfers, and the rest is history.

While on the subject of Tucson golf courses, I must tell about a humorous incident that occurred at the old El Rio Country Club.

In front of the sixth tee was a small lake, over which the players had to drive the ball. Many balls ended up in the bottom of the lake, rather than on the fairway on the other side of the lake.

One of the club's most ardent golfers was a fellow by the name of Homer Boyd, who was, at one time, chairman of the County Board of Supervisors. He operated a drugstore on the southwest corner of Campbell Avenue and Sixth Street. It was popular with the golfers of El Rio, with whom he enjoyed playing.

He was redheaded, and not without reason. He had a quick temper, particularly when the results of his efforts on the golf course did not turn out to his satisfaction. One time when we were playing, he hit a ball into the lake on the sixth hole. He teed up another ball, which also ended up in the lake. With that, he picked up his bag of clubs, which was being carried by a small caddy, and threw them into the lake. Then, after he cooled down a bit, he wanted the caddy to go in after them. When the caddy refused, he pushed the poor guy into the lake. Then he jumped in himself and pulled out both the caddy and golf bag, amidst much laughter. He was a good-natured fellow most of the time, but he never did live down that incident.

Golf Pros—And Cons

IT IS NOT generally known, but the very first golf series made for and shown on television were made in Arizona at the Tucson Country Club and the Phoenix Country Club.

A TV producer named DeMets from Chicago had been successful for several years in producing a series of special shows about bowling. During the winter months, when people in most parts of the nation were confined to indoor activities, DeMets had found that people enjoyed watching a sporting activity such as bowling. He arranged special matches between the better-known professional bowlers and was successful in selling the series to TV stations.

At that time, there was a travel agent by the name of Lolita Lynn who operated an agency in Chicago known as Arizona In Chicago. She knew our state well and represented many of the better resorts such as Camelback Inn, Mountain Shadows, Arizona Inn, Lodge on the Desert, the El Conquistador, and many guest ranches. She was aggressive and creative. When I was managing the Tucson Sunshine Climate Club, Tucson's prime tourist promotion organization, I worked closely with her.

DeMets had contacted Lynn to see if she knew of some place in Arizona that might be interested in joining him in developing a trial balloon on a series of golf matches. She called me and I told her that it sounded very interesting, but I would have to check on golf clubs in Tucson and Phoenix to ascertain their willingness to permit the golf matches to be played and photographed at the Tucson and Phoenix Country Clubs, which, at that time, were our best golf settings.

The Phoenix group was enthusiastic about the project, but George Amos, president of the Tucson Country Club and not a particularly enthusiastic golfer, was hesitant. However, when some of us put pressure on him, he agreed to permit five of the matches to be played and photographed at the Tucson Country Club. The other eight matches were made in Phoenix.

Several of us watched some of the locally made matches, which included such top players as Cary Middlecoff, Jimmy Demaret, Lloyd Mangram, Byron Nelson, Jug McSpadden, Ed Furgol, Tommy Bolt, and others. No one knew what the reaction would be because golf games had never before been shown regularly on TV.

They proved to be very popular, and country clubs all over the nation began bidding to have matches made at their club. Tucson Country Club didn't realize the value of having their golf course shown on TV screens all over the world and even ended up charging DeMets a few hundred dollars to pay for repairs to one of the fairways they claimed was damaged. That finished Tucson as a site for further golf series, unfortunately.

But Arizona was the location for the beginning of golf tournaments on television, which today are so popular. Up until then, only a flash of an important tournament would be shown on news programs. Shell's Wonderful World of Golf was soon being produced and shown worldwide, as were other golf series.

Another of my interesting experiences with golf involved a famous golfer and renowned gambler. He never was a professional golfer, though he played well enough to be one. However, he felt he could do better being less well known and taking money away from unsuspecting chumps who thought they were world beaters.

His name was Ty Thomas, but he was better known by the glamorous title of Titanic Thompson. He'd been written up by nearly every sportswriter who ever lived and in nearly every sports magazine ever published. *Sports Illustrated* even ran a series of three articles about him and his exploits.

Ty was a good enough golfer to play with the best professionals and gamble for big stakes, either with players or with backers who would bet heavily on them. I'm speaking of Byron Nelson, Jimmy Demaret, Jog McSpadden, Lloyd Mangram, Paul Runyon, and others of that era. But in addition to being a crack golfer, he also was a champion trapshooter, a fearless card player, and a very crafty gambler at almost any game. He was known as a "proposition bettor," which meant that he would conceive all kinds of games and things to bet on and always had the best of it, one way or another.

Ty didn't play for the sport of it—he played to win. That was the way he made a living, by his wits. I don't think he was ever in any kind of legitimate business.

He lived in Tucson for eight or ten years back in the late '30s and early '40s. I got acquainted with him hanging around Dooley's and other pool halls where we'd go to watch pool and billiard games on which large amounts of money were bet. He was a friendly fellow, although he seldom smiled. He nearly always carried with him some kind of valuable jewelry, an expensive watch or diamond ring or necklace he'd offer to sell at a real bargain price. Where it came from always remained a mystery, but we all imagined he was fencing it for a friend.

In those days, there was some kind of a gambling joint in every town in Arizona. When the gamblers who ran those outfits learned that the famous Titanic Thompson was in Tucson, they would come here nearly every week just to spend time with him, listen to his latest propositions, and get in on some action. They'd play cards, shoot craps, pitch pennies, play pool and billiards, and do almost anything to test their skills against an internationally known champion.

They'd come to Tucson on Mondays from Phoenix, Mesa, Miami and Globe, Bisbee, Yuma, and even from Prescott and Flagstaff. They'd usually gather at the El Rio Country Club where they'd often get involved in some kind of a Mickey Mouse golf game in which Ty would give them two or three shots a hole on a five-hole match. He'd invariably beat them, so they'd finally catch on and refuse to play any kind of a golf game with him.

One Monday he proposed that the seven of them who were at El Rio that day play a hole with a hammer. "Anyone can hit a ball with a hammer," he told them, then got a hammer and had them try it. Sure enough, each of them found out he could hit a golf ball with a hammer. They agreed to play the first hole at El Rio with a hammer for a $1,000 bet each.

Ty sent Slim, the bartender, to a hardware store to buy seven hammers. They each teed up a ball on the first tee and hit it down the fairway. They continued to hit the ball until they got it into the cup—winner take all. Needless to say, Ty was the winner by a mile, and had earned a week's salary, at least.

A week later I asked him how long he had been practicing hitting a ball with a hammer, to which he replied, "Oh, about two weeks." He always had the best of it when he put his dough on the line, especially with unsuspecting chumps such as those who gathered to see him on Mondays in Tucson.

Every winter the Tucson Trap and Skeet Club has an annual shooting event that attracts people from all over the nation to compete for various trophies, but especially for the State Championship Cup, which goes to the man with the highest score. Champions from several states always come to Tucson to enjoy the good weather and try to add the Arizona title to their trophies.

No one wanted to compete against Titanic Thompson, of course. But he was entitled to take part, and did, and won both times he competed. Ty was not only cagey but also was very skillful at a lot of things.

He told me the only time he was arrested and spent time in jail was while he was in Tucson. He had gotten dates with some young ladies for a couple of visiting friends. One of the girls was badly abused by one of Ty's friends and when it was discovered she was only seventeen, the police picked up Ty and held him for a few days during the investigation. He was released after a few days, but he never got over the fact that he had been locked up for the only time in his life.

Ty was a tall, angular guy who played golf left-handed but could also play quite well right-handed if he had to. He didn't use foul language and was always a cool gentleman.

Now, for my personal experience with Ty. The gamblers who gathered on Monday in Tucson called me one day the week before and asked if I would be willing to play golf with him the following Monday. At that time, my handicap was 2, and I had twice been the Tucson City Champion in recent years. I had heard about some of the town's better golfers' playing matches with him. I thought it would be fun, but I told them I didn't want to know anything about the bets that were to be made. I was certain that Ty would know about my ability as a golfer and would adjust the bets by giving me strokes but I didn't want to know anything about it—and I was not informed.

On the first tee, Ty asked me if I'd like to have a little five-dollar Nassau bet that could result in my losing no more than twenty dollars. I felt it was worth that much to play with the famous guy. I accepted the bet, although I knew I had little chance of winning.

At the end of the first nine, I was one down. On the back nine, the gamblers asked me to wait to tee off while they gathered to "to do some business." At the end of the seventeenth hole, I was one down on the back side and the boys asked for a short recess while they had a meeting with Ty to discuss some more business. Finally, we teed off on the last hole, which is a rather short five par one.

Up until then, Ty had been outdriving me by ten to twenty yards. I was never a long hitter. But after all the bets were down on the eighteenth hole, Ty outdrove me by at least fifty yards. His second shot was about 250 yards and landed on the green, assuring him of a birdie. I was still some fifty or sixty yards short of the green after my second shot. I hit a good approach and left myself about fifteen or twenty feet from the cup. Ty putted up for a gimme on his third shot. I had to sink my lengthy putt for a tie, which I failed to do.

I don't know how much the gamblers lost to Ty, but I know I paid him twenty dollars and felt I got my money's worth.

People

Early Tucson Characters

Tucson had a cast of strange, humorous—and some pitiful—characters who used to roam our streets and add a bit of color to our old downtown area. Some of them got their names when they came aboard our whirling world, whereas others inherited their names from those who saw them as unusual people.

One of the most colorful characters was known as Alkali Ike. He was a large man who always sported a beard, which was unusual for men in those days. He lived down on the southeast side of the city but was often seen almost anywhere in the downtown district, especially along South Meyer Street, where various small businesses operated as mom-and-pop concerns. It was also home to one or two larger stores, as well as Chinese grocery stores, a couple of meat markets, and several saloons.

Alkali Ike always wore bib overalls and was fond of talking to himself out loud as he walked along. He was considered to be harmless and, as far as I knew, was. He claimed to be an expert mechanic and often had grease on his overalls, his hands, and his face. Everybody knew him. He was friendly and seemed always to show up if there was an accident or an incident that attracted any kind of attention or a crowd, such as a fire alarm.

I remember one time when they were paving South Meyer, a mule team working on the job became excited over something. One of the mules kicked a workman in the head and killed him. Of course, a small crowd quickly gathered—Alkali Ike right in the middle of it, claiming he could revive the man if we all turned our backs and allowed him to do some magic he claimed he knew. Everyone turned his back, but we peeked over our shoulders to see what he would do. He never touched the guy but only went through some strange motions with his hands while chanting some passages from the Bible. The poor soul lying in the street remained dead. Alkali Ike didn't do him any harm, but he sure didn't do him any good.

Another time I saw Ike in a small crowd gathered around a wagon that had broken down on the street. Some men were trying to remove a wheel from it, but a nut that held the wheel in place was too tight for them. After a while, Alkali Ike spoke up and said that he could get it off. When one of the workmen told Ike he would welcome his help, Ike said, "The only way to get it off is to bite it off." This caused a ripple of laughter. Ike got down and actually tried to bite the nut, which caused even more laughter. Someone remarked that he had never before seen one nut biting another.

One short, black gentleman known as the "Major," who lived on the north side, would come around in the early evenings, very neatly decked out in a black swallowtail coat, tuxedo shirt, bow tie, and no less than a stovepipe hat. Sometimes he would show up wearing a large belt with a sword in a scabbard hanging from it. He claimed to be a veteran of the Civil War who had served under some unknown major, about whom he spoke often. He was often the butt of jokes or tricks by unthinking people.

One of the most interesting and useful characters found on Tucson streets in the early days was the Greek popcorn man who had a regular spot on the northeast corner of Stone Avenue and Congress Street. He was a short, dumpy gentleman who had a handlebar mustache and always wore a felt hat. Every evening at dusk, he would come down Congress Street pushing his glass-enclosed popcorn wagon. He would park it in the gutter on the Stone Avenue side of the corner, light up his gas burner, and start popping popcorn. That was all he sold, but it smelled so good, few people could resist buying a bag, so he sold a lot of it.

George, as he was known, carried on his business at that stand for thirty years or more. He raised his family and supported them as the only popcorn maker in town.

Pepper Carpentier was another real character who was a very useful and worthwhile citizen. He was somewhat misshapen, and stood only about four foot eight. He had been a "news butcher," or news-boy, in some city back east but had come to Tucson for the health of his daughter. He not only sold papers to get started here, but he had brought with him a tremendously large megaphone that was taller than he was.

To add to his income, he became the town crier, standing at busy downtown intersections announcing all kinds of commercial events, such as openings of new restaurants, special sales at department stores, and so forth.

It wasn't long before everybody in town knew Pepper. He literally built a business from scratch. He would attend all sporting events and tell the world about whatever he was promoting at the time. He was never offensive but would enthusiastically peddle the wares of those who paid him to do so.

While I was managing the Fox Theater, I hired him almost on a weekly basis to spread the word about our upcoming movies and such things as Bank Night or car giveaways. For a good twenty years, until his death in 1948, Pepper was a worthwhile part of the local scene.

Another character, somewhat less colorful than others around town, was a slight Mexican-American man by the name of Donisio Mesa. He would wander the streets, never bothering anyone, and was very friendly—especially if you could speak a little Spanish. He always carried a cut-down pool cue with him. He had the knack of being able to use it as a seat by somehow folding his legs so he could sit by the hour on it.

He frequently would come and prop himself up in front of the old Opera House when I was managing it. I would often let him see the movie. He couldn't understand English, but he said he always liked to see the pretty girls and listen to the music. He was one of our town's best girl-watchers.

He had a good sense of humor and I used to tease him about girls leaving a message for him with the cashier of the theater. Once I told him in Spanish that I knew of a house where he could get a taco, a bottle of beer, and a lady all for three dollars. His eyes lit up and he asked, actually pleaded with me, asking, "¿Dónde? ¿Dónde?"

When I told him I wouldn't tell him, he replied, "Okay, Mr. Drachman. I'm going to look it up in the Yellow Pages."

We had another, less savory, girl-watcher who used to roam our downtown streets, especially on days when the wind would swirl around the corner of Stone and Congress and blow skirts up a bit. The interesting thing about this man was that he was in his fifties and was always well dressed. He wore a hat like the one made popular years later by Bear Bryant. He performed his little tricks for years but didn't fool any of us who watched his antics.

He was not just a looker but also a toucher, who would rub the back of his hand up against a woman's bottom as she waited for the traffic light to change. Many of us guys knew what he was up to but he was pretty restrained so it was hard to pin anything on him, although once in a while a woman would turn around and stare him into retreating.

A movie theater was always a place where many different kinds of characters would be attracted. Former theatrical people were always colorful and fun to be around—or at least I enjoyed them.

There was one unforgettable woman from Philadelphia who operated a theatrical rooming and boarding house where actors, Vaudevillians, press agents, and managers used to stay. She told a story about a theater man, and her fellow Philadelphian, by the name of Joe Rickards, who had come to Arizona a few years before for his health. In Phoenix, he and a man named Harry Nace started the Rickards & Nace chain of theaters, which at one time owned about twenty movie theaters in Arizona. They came to Tucson and formed a company with my father and his partner, Ben Goldsmith. I knew both Rickards and Nace very well.

The lady from Philadelphia, who was named Mrs. Heller, or Ma Heller as she referred to herself, told a funny story about Rickards, one that was hard to believe but which she swore was true.

When Rickards's health deteriorated to the point that doctors told him he had to go Arizona if he wanted to live—he was tubercular— the theatrical people he knew in Philadelphia generously contributed to a fund to pay for his trip and give him a few bucks to get started in Phoenix. Ma Heller said that a few months later, a telegram was received from someone who claimed he was a friend of Rickards's, advising them that Joe Rickards had died and that $300 was needed to cover the funeral expenses. She said that his former friends wired the money to Rickards's friend, only to learn several months later that Joe Rickards was indeed alive and joking about how he made suckers out of the bunch of theatrical people in Philly.

One afternoon in the summer when I was working in the office of the Opera House, Ma Heller was sitting with Ben Goldsmith on a settee in the lobby right outside the office door visiting about the day's events. A preacher came to the office and asked me if the Opera

House would contribute ten dollars to an orphans' fund his church was sponsoring.

I told him I'd have to ask Ben Goldsmith. He and I stepped out of the office to the settee where Ben and Ma Heller were sitting. The preacher made his pitch and Ben said to give him ten dollars, which I did. Then the preacher turned to Ma Heller and started to tell *her* about all the orphans who needed help.

Before he finished his sad story, she interrupted him and gave him an answer I've never forgotten. It went like this: "If more of you men buttoned your pants in back like you do your collar, there wouldn't be so many orphans in the world." The preacher blinked and made a hasty retreat.

Tucson Police in the '20s and '30s

TUCSON IN THE 1920s and 1930s was a fairly peaceful town. Of course it wasn't crime free, but there weren't nearly the number of serious crimes we see now.

We had an efficient police department that handled the petty crimes without much fanfare, although once in a while the newspapers would latch onto a case they thought would build readership.

One of the principal sources of crime was Prohibition. Because so many people didn't sympathize with the law, it wasn't always strictly enforced by local law officers except in flagrant cases by professional bootleggers.

Drugs, as we know them today, were practically unheard of. The few people who were known to use "dope," as it was called, were spoken of as "hop heads" and looked down upon. Marijuana was rarely used and, again, those who used it were frowned upon.

I remember that in 1922, while I was in high school, for some reason or other the editor of the *Tucson Citizen* got into a beef with the chief of police, who I believe at the time was either Dallas Ford or Jack Dyer, both long-time and well-respected police officers.

The editor of the *Citizen* was a man by the name of Lyons. His daughter was in one of my classes at Tucson High. Editor Lyons claimed that the sale of dope in Tucson was rampant. He also claimed that the Tucson Police Department was aware of the source of the dope but was doing nothing about it.

This became a hot issue. Daily, the *Citizen* would make new charges about the police chief's lack of attention to the ready availability of drugs.

Finally, one day the editor of the *Citizen* claimed that he could make a single phone call and have a Western Union messenger deliver a package of dope to his office. He even invited the police chief to come witness the delivery. Furthermore, he said, the chief was being paid off by the head of the syndicate that was running dope here from Mexico.

These were serious charges and had people talking all over town. When the police chief refused to accept his invitation, Editor Lyons challenged the mayor instead to come to his office at a certain time the following week so he could prove his "single phone call" claim.

The Mayor accepted the invitation. Editor Lyons made his phone call and presto, within half an hour, a Western Union messenger delivered a small package of dope to his office.

This, of course, was very damaging to the police chief and his entire force. Lyons gloated in his columns and demanded investigations by the county attorney's office.

About ten days later, the then-owners of the *Citizen* announced that Editor Lyons had resigned and moved out of the state. This was a real shocker to the community. The *Citizen* was silent as to what happened, but word eventually got around that during the time that Editor Lyons was making the allegations about the local police, a very attractive woman had appealed to the campaigning editor to allow her to tell him a sad tale about her mother and child who had come to Tucson for their health and had practically no resources to live on.

She had called on Lyons and asked for his help with one of the welfare agencies. She saw him several times and finally invited him to come to her apartment to meet the mother and daughter. He accepted.

The story went that when he showed up at the apartment, the young woman was in a negligee, waiting for him. She soon had him in her bed. Out of a closet stepped a photographer who captured a flash picture of Editor Lyons in the buff and in a most compromising situation.

Police were handy and moved in. That was end of the *Citizen*'s campaign to run the police chief out of town. Whether the police had trapped him or not made no difference—the campaigning editor was long gone.

I was just a high school kid, but even people my age knew that something strange had suddenly taken place. Lyons's daughter disappeared from class and hasn't been heard from since.

The police force in those days was made up of local men who were well respected. Besides Dallas Ford and Jack Dyer, the list of good guys included Mark Robbins, the fingerprint expert, Ben West, Jesús Camacho, Jay Smith—our first motorcycle cop—Pancho Franco, Harry Leslie, Charley Hines, Swede Walker, Ed Faustman, Chet Sherman, Frank Eyman, Gus Wollard, Jimmy Hearon, Tom Burke, and a few others. Sergeant McLaughlin presided for a time over the "front office" as desk sergeant.

Jesús Camacho was one of the most popular of all the officers. He was a big guy who always wore a large western hat. He would often ride around town on a white horse. The kids all loved him. He knew every bad guy in town and he usually provided quick answers to strange petty crimes. Between Camacho and Franco, not much went on in the underworld that they weren't aware of.

One time, in about 1924 or '25, Camacho caught a big fish that brought him national recognition as a police officer. There had been a grisly murder in Los Angeles of a woman by another woman who was accused of killing her victim in a love triangle. She had used a carpenter's hammer to beat her to death. The name of the murderess was Clara Phillips, and she had mysteriously disappeared. Police all over California were frantically searching for the "Hammer Murderer."

One bright Tucson morning, Jesús Camacho, acting on a tip, searched a Southern Pacific train when it pulled into the station, and he collared Clara. Camacho's picture was spread over the front pages of newspapers throughout the nation.

Having arrested the famous Hammer Murderer from Los Angeles, the Tucson Police Department received new respect from the local press and citizenry.

One of the officers who was held in high regard by the public and other officers on the force was Charley Hines, who, not long after joining the department, was assigned the special task of finding a thief who had recently been conducting a series of home burglaries in the near north side, around Speedway and North Sixth Avenue. He was bold, and his armed robberies had neighbors scared as hell.

Charley Hines was patrolling an alley in the area on foot one night when he spotted a man who answered the description of the burglar. The man was about half a block away. When Charley shouted at him to halt and identified himself as a police officer, the burglar drew a gun, fired at Charley, and ran.

Charley ran after him. When the thief got into a lighted area, Charley fired a shot and killed him instantly. That put an end to the north-side crime spree and established Charley Hines as one of Tucson's best police officers.

A few years later, while I was running the Fox Theater, an armed man held up our cashier and got away with about ninety dollars. The cashier was scared to death. Police responded, but the thief was long gone, though the cashier gave them a good description of him.

During the next week, a man answering that description robbed a grocery store and a service station, and many businesspeople were nervous and frightened. The police were on the alert, and the guy's description ran in the papers.

A few nights later, I was standing in front of the Fox when a volley of shots, loud as a gun battle, rang out. And a gun battle was exactly what was going on across Congress Street in the Western Union office, right next to the Valley National Bank.

All of a sudden, the gunfire stopped and was replaced by complete quiet. Soon a police car arrived in front of the Western Union, and officers rushed inside.

By that time, a few of us were bold enough to approach the Western Union. Three or four officers were inside, and the air was gray with smoke. One of the cops spotted me and motioned me in. He took me to a man lying on the floor, badly wounded, bleeding from his mouth and from various wounds. He obviously was dying.

The officers wanted to see if I could identify him as the man who had robbed the Fox. I told them I couldn't but that I would get the cashier. I brought her over and when she looked at the dying man, she said he was, indeed, the one who had held her up.

We soon learned that when he'd come into the Western Union, one of the women working near the back had thought he was acting a little strangely. She called the police station. Charley Hines and another officer responded, coming in through the back door.

Just as they arrived, the burglar made his move. He pulled his gun and demanded the cash in the drawers. Charley stepped out into the office and identified himself as police, only to draw shots from the thief.

As the burglar jumped behind a desk, Charley and the other officer fired back and a real gun battle was on. Charley maneuvered into a position from which he had a clear shot at the bad guy, and took him out.

None of this could compare to what happened the next year, of course, when the local police arrested, without firing a shot, John Dillinger and three of his notorious gang. But that story has been told many times, and I'll not repeat it here.

Epes Randolph and Three Railroad Lines

DURING THE FORTY or so years after 1880, Tucson was filled with news of three railroad lines, each of which played an important role in the Old Pueblo.

The Southern Pacific Railroad Line was the first one to come to town, in 1880, and had a tremendous impact on the community. It opened up to Tucson fairly rapid delivery of freight and opportunities for passengers to reach the isolated, tiny city in relative comfort.

One item in particular that my grandmother told me was important was the ice, which could be brought to Tucsonans for the first time and was available for families who shortly thereafter acquired ice boxes.

The Southern Pacific was the only line serving Tucson until about 1915, when the El Paso & Southwestern Railroad Line was built from El Paso into Tucson and west to San Diego. I well remember going as a youngster with my father to watch the line being constructed just east of the Santa Cruz River.

The company built its station, part of which still stands, on West Congress Street. It was one of the most beautiful buildings in Tucson and, although it has not been used as a railroad station for some time, it has served many purposes in our community over the years. Today it houses a restaurant, Carlos Murphy's.

In order to reach San Diego, the line had to run into Mexico part of the way. The brakeman on the train would have to open a metal gate and let the train into Mexico and then, as it approached the U.S. border again, open another to permit the train to continue on its way to the West Coast. This line was used by trains to Los Angeles well into the 1930s.

The El Paso & Southwestern Line was competitive with the Southern Pacific for a few years, but the Southern Pacific, with its connection with the Rock Island Railroad, provided superior service to Chicago and other midwestern cities. It eventually bought out and absorbed the El Paso and Southwestern.

Around 1910, a man by the name of Epes Randolph, who had been connected with the Southern Pacific Railroad for many years and was considered one of the more important business executives in the Southwest, put together investors from the East Coast and developed the Southern Pacific de México.

This line started in Tucson, running south through Nogales and on down to the West Coast to Empalme, Mexico, to the Guaymas area, and on further south to the rich agricultural areas that have, for many years, produced vegetables for the U.S. markets.

Epes Randolph was an outstanding citizen of Tucson. He was the man who gave 480 acres of land at the southwest corner of Broadway and Alvernon Road to the City of Tucson, providing it would create a park. This, of course, was named Randolph Park and soon became central to the life of the community—as it still is today.

Head offices for the Southern Pacific de México were set up in Tucson. There were forty or fifty people employed in these, which represented quite an economic boon to the Old Pueblo in those days.

After a time, the offices were moved from Tucson to Empalme, which created considerable unhappiness in town because quite a few families either lost their jobs or had to move to Mexico. I had an aunt, Esther Drachman, who had to make the move to Empalme. She soon came back home to Tucson, however.

For many years, the Southern Pacific Railroad was the largest employer in Tucson. Wages paid to engineers and firemen were among the top in the city. A Southern Pacific engineer was considered to be a very fortunate man; he had a steady income and lived well. At one time, the Southern Pacific even built a row of about twenty-five houses along South Third Avenue especially for its engineers and firemen. This created one of the most attractive and stable residential areas in the early days of Tucson.

The Southern Pacific also sponsored a baseball team, managed by Mike Robles, which for quite a while was the leading ball club in town. I played on that team as the shortstop for several years. My only other gringo teammate was the second baseman, Joe Wagner. All the rest of the team was composed of either Indian or Mexican ballplayers, who were pretty darn good, as well as a nice group of people to be around. We played games against teams from Phoenix, Casa Grande, Bisbee, Douglas, Miami-Globe, and Nogales. Sometimes army teams from Mexico would come up and play us.

I remember that we had an excellent pitcher who was an Indian who had come from Mexico. He liked to drink tequila, and almost every weekend he would get plastered. He was our best pitcher, so when we had an important Sunday game, we would have the police pick him up on Saturday night and keep him overnight so that we could go to the jail on Sunday morning and find a sober pitcher. It wasn't the nicest thing for us to do but we won a few ball games that way.

I know that the name of Randolph Park has been changed to Reid Park in some areas. Since that happened, I've wondered if there might be a clause in the grant from Epes Randolph to the city stating that the land would revert to the estate if the name of the park were ever changed. I don't know if there are any relatives of Epes Randolph left (I don't believe there are any here), but if there are, I imagine they might be able to generate some pretty interesting activity in court.

When Epes Randolph died, I attended the funeral services at the Masonic Temple on South Scott Street. There was no room inside, so hundreds of us had to stand on the outside: his funeral was, without doubt, the largest one held in Tucson for many years.

The Weekender and Malachy Hynes

IN 1933, IN the midst of the recession, a health-seeking Irish newspaper reporter from Dublin began publishing a tabloid-size weekly newspaper he called the *Tucson Weekender*. The publisher was Malachy Hynes. He'd been here for about a year and had become a good friend of mine while I was managing the Opera House, one of the Old Pueblo's three movie theaters. Newspaper people and theater people have an affinity for each other, and it was common for reporters and others of the fourth estate to find their way to my office at the Opera House.

Malachy Hynes was a most pleasant guy with strong opinions about the English and the injustices he claimed they had committed against his country and its citizens. He was a member of the Irish underground movement and, although he was obviously not a robust man, he had a spirit that could make him a dangerous enemy if a situation called for it. He was tubercular, as were many people who came to our town, but he was not so ill that he couldn't live a fairly normal life. He was employed as a reporter by one of the local newspapers for a while, but his assignments were not to his liking, so he decided to devote his talents to producing a newspaper of his own.

He began by printing and distributing 3,000 copies on green newsprint, the Irishman's native color. He wouldn't get rich from his new venture, but it could and did provide him a meager living, which is all he needed because he was receiving some help from his family overseas.

The *Tucson Weekender* was unlike any publication ever seen in Tucson. Malachy wrote every word of every story. He had become acquainted with many well-known local people and concocted all kinds of nutty stories about them, most without a word of truth but harmlessly humorous. He would use head shots of important international people over the name of one or another of those local figures. That only increased circulation, and the *Weekender* was a hit.

Although the small neighborhood of Menlo Park, which is located west of the Santa Cruz River and just north of West Congress Street, was barely ever newsworthy, the *Weekender* made it sound as if it were an important community in which something vitally interesting was happening almost weekly. For instance, while John Dillinger was in the local hoosegow, the top headline read, "John Dillinger to speak at Elks frolic tonight at Menlo Park." The story said that at the massed civic whoopee, a statue of Mae West was to be unveiled and that the lord mayors of Menlo Park, Jack Mulcahy and Sparkie Webber, would preside. Garbo and Ghandi were among visiting nobility invited. (Of course, Mulcahy and Webber, local businessmen, were not officeholders in Menlo Park, nor was anyone else.)

Depending on the subject, Malachy would identify himself as the Cow Editor, Blessed Event Editor, or editor of any one of the following, all of which appeared during the editions of 1933: Cuisine, Assault & Battery, Socialite, Pediatrics, Aeronautics, Ethereal, Mob-Scene, Up & At 'Em, Thespian, Histrionics, Neighborly, Divine Comedy, Thither & Yon, Pandemonium, Pot Pourri, Pomp & Circumstance, Autobiographical, Chronological, Therapeutics, and a few others.

I've shown my collected three-years' worth of *Tucson Weekenders*, which I have bound in large books, to young people who live here, and each says it must have been great fun living in Tucson at that time.

And they're right: it *was* a lot of fun being here in the mid-thirties, even if we were in the depths of the Great Depression.

The *Tucson Weekender* survived for most of four years because Malachy did all the work, including selling all its advertising. The paper was full of ads for restaurants, movie theaters, nightclubs, and other businesses that were not part of the Tucson Retail Merchants Association, which designated the publications in which members could advertise. He had a four-year feud with that group. They never did approve his paper as an acceptable publication. He struggled but survived anyway.

The collection of *Tucson Weekenders* that I have is really a treasure trove showing what an alternative newspaper could be. It was like the *New Yorker* only never as serious. One of the local newspapers could have enough material from them to fill a weekly column for years. I'll turn them over to the Arizona Historical Society one of these days. They can serve as a memorial to a humorous, feisty Irish newspaper man who made a stop in Tucson on his way to heaven, where he must now be the editor of Saint Peter's newspaper.

My Friend Justice William O. Douglas

ONE OF MY most unforgettable and certainly one of my most important friends was William O. Douglas, who served as a member of the U.S. Supreme Court for many years.

He would have been president of the United States if he said yes when, in 1944, President Franklin D. Roosevelt asked him to run with him as his vice presidential candidate. Roosevelt had appointed Douglas to the court a few years before that and held him in high esteem.

After Douglas turned down the vice presidency, Roosevelt selected Senator Harry Truman, who became president upon Roosevelt's death a year later.

Bill Douglas grew up in the state of Washington and was a true outdoorsman. He spent a lot of time climbing mountains, riding horses, and enjoying the great outdoors in general, not only in America but in other places around the world. In the early '50s, Bill had a terrible accident in his home state, when a horse he was riding on a narrow trail fell and rolled over on him, fracturing a great many of his ribs. He nearly died.

After he was released from the hospital, he came to Tucson to

Left to right Jack Sakrison of Valley National Bank, Justice William O. Douglas, and Roy. *Arizona Historical Society.*

recuperate in our good winter climate. It was late fall. Several of his friends in the East had gotten busy, calling contacts in Tucson to alert them of his arrival here. I had calls from two friends in Washington, D.C., telling me about him and the fact that he was going to remain here for several months. They pointed out that his salary as an associate justice did not provide him with the kind of income needed to stay at one of our expensive guest ranches. Therefore, they hoped that somehow a place could be found on a ranch, rather than in town, where he could recuperate.

At that time, I was managing a small ranch property in the Tanque Verde area for my close friend, New Yorker Bill Becker, who owned one of the largest photographic galleries in the world. For years he had a contract with Sears Roebuck to take all the fashion pictures for their huge catalog, which was produced several times each year.

Becker had brought his party of photographers, technicians and a bevy of beautiful models here. They spent two ten-week periods in Tucson each year, so he and I got to be close friends. He'd constructed a good-sized swimming pool with two buildings on each side. Two of them were bedrooms; one served as a kitchen, dining room, and living room; and the third was a film laboratory in which his technicians would process the day's films.

I called Becker in New York and told him about Justice Douglas's wanting to stay at his Tucson ranch for a few months. He knew that Douglas was a very liberal guy and jokingly said that it would be okay as long as he didn't sport redneck ties.

I called Douglas at the Triple H Ranch on Wilmot Road, where he was staying, and made a date to pick him up and show him Becker's ranch. When I arrived at the Triple H, he was sitting in front waiting for me. He introduced Mrs. Douglas, who was going to drive a station wagon full of clothes and bags. Douglas was to drive a four-door car, also loaded with clothes. They followed me to Becker's ranch on Speedway, ready to move in.

When we arrived at Becker's, we walked around the buildings and, while they were looking at them, I excused myself and told them I would go to the caretaker's to get the keys so we could get inside.

When I got back, the justice was climbing in one of the windows, which he had "jimmied." I laughed and said that I wished I had a camera to take a picture of a justice of the Supreme Court breaking and entering. It was quite apparent that he was an easy guy to be around, especially after he told me then to call him Bill.

He immediately said he would appreciate the opportunity to stay there. They unloaded the cars and moved in.

Bill made a deal with the caretaker's wife for her to prepare meals for them and to do the housekeeping while they were there. His wife, Mildred, stayed at the ranch only a couple of days and returned home. This was the beginning of their separation and, later, their divorce.

Bill invited me to have dinner with him on many occasions. I certainly enjoyed his company and that of his many prominent visitors who came here during his three-month stay. I saw him four or five times a week, generally in the evenings.

His guests included several federal judges from the Ninth Circuit Court of Appeals, over which Bill exerted considerable power, as did the other Supreme Court justices over their court domains. One of his most important visitors was Supreme Court justice Hugo Black, who stayed three or four days here with him. I spent a couple of evenings with them during that time, which was exciting to me.

One visitor I particularly remember was Sol Haas, who was from

Seattle, where he owned several radio stations and a television station. He was an ardent and powerful Democrat. Bill told me that it was largely through Haas's efforts that the president had appointed him to the Supreme Court. He stayed with Bill for a couple of weeks and we became good friends.

One evening after Bill had gone to bed, as he usually did about nine o'clock under doctor's orders, I asked Sol about his role in having the president appoint Bill to the Court. He said it was easy, because Roosevelt already held Douglas in high regard while he was chairman of the Securities and Exchange Commission.

He said he had made an appointment to see the president and that when he sat down across the desk from President Roosevelt, he asked him if he had a bottle of Scotch handy, which the President promptly produced. After a couple of drinks and a short discussion about politics, he said he made the proposal that Bill Douglas would be an excellent member of the U.S. Supreme Court. The president said he would give him serious consideration.

Sol told me he then called on several senators and other Washington officials and urged them to write President Roosevelt endorsing the Douglas candidacy. He got the job done. Bill was appointed.

Bill had friends all over the world. One evening, for example, the phone rang and he asked me to answer it. It was a call from a Mr. Palavi, who happened to be the Shah of Iran. He was calling to check on the health of his friend, Judge Douglas.

One night after Bill had gone to bed, Sol and I continued to drink and discuss events of the day. About eleven o'clock, Sol said, "Let's go wake up Bill and tell him what we think of what's going on in the world." When I tried to deter him, he said, "Aw, come on, he gets too much sleep anyway." When we entered the room, Sol turned on the light and told Bill that there were a couple of drunks here to see him. Bill sat up and asked, "Who are they, and what do they want?"

Sol told him it was Sol and Roy and that we wanted to know how he felt. Bill promptly told us to get lost and let him sleep.

Bill finished his first book, *Of Men and Mountains,* while he was here. He had two of his girlfriends come to Tucson for a visit (not at the same time, of course). They helped him edit the manuscript.

One of these ladies was a real beauty. Her name was Frances, and she and I became good friends. We kept in touch for many years. She said that the book should be titled *Of Men and Mountings,* referring to Bill's proclivity for romantic affairs.

Nearly every year after Bill returned to the Court, he would spend his spring vacation here in Tucson. He generally stayed at the De la Osa ranch, located on the Mexican border near Sasabe. Dick Jenkins ran it as a working ranch that also took guests.

Bill wasn't much interested in clothes or fashions. One day he called me from De la Osa and asked me to meet him at the Pioneer Hotel, where he would be spending the night. He arrived in the same khaki clothes he had been wearing at the ranch. He had a large duffel bag with him from which he pulled a very wrinkled suit that he put on before we were to meet some friends for dinner. He looked like hell, but it didn't bother him one bit.

One evening in my living room, we got to talking about drinking. Three or four of his visitors, all men, were there and were talking about heavy drinking and some of its bad effects. Bill said that once he was a pretty good drinker and could hold his liquor better than most people. He told of a drinking contest he and a group of friends conducted once on a hunting trip.

He said they a created a pool of money and started drinking booze, with each one drinking the same amount. It was agreed that they would continue until all but one passed out. Bill said that as each reached the stage of stupor, he was laid down in front of the fireplace in the cabin. He claimed proudly that he was the only one who remained upright as the evening wore on. He was the champ and won the pot.

After Bill recovered his health and returned to his duties on the Court, I dropped in on him several times in Washington. He was always glad to see me. I visited his chambers and sat in on a couple of appeals before the Court. It was an exciting experience for me, sitting there and being recognized by Bill from the Supreme Court bench with a smile and a bow of his head.

While I was president of the American Society of Real Estate Counselors in the late '60s, our midwinter meeting was held in Washington. Mrs. Drachman and I hosted a cocktail party for some 150 people who were members of the organization at one of the downtown hotels. I called Bill a day or two before and asked if he would like to come to the party, which was a black-tie affair.

Bill not only accepted the invitation, he arrived early so we could have a visit and then stood in the reception line along with us, greeting the members as they arrived. They were impressed that I was able to get a justice from the U.S. Supreme Court to attend our party, but Bill loved people and said he enjoyed himself.

On another occasion when I was in Washington, as a member of the Realtors' Washington Committee, the lobbying organization for the National Association of Realtors, I and other members of the committee invited members of the House of Representatives and the senators from each of our respective states to attend a fancy "Congressional Dinner" that was held each year to foster legislation we felt was important.

I called Bill when I arrived in town and I asked him if he would accept an invitation to our dinner. He said he'd be happy to do so. When I asked the chairman of the dinner if they had ever had a member of the Supreme Court attend one of these large affairs, he replied they had not. When I told him I could get Justice Douglas to attend, he was excited and told me to be sure to invite him, which I did.

Bill was the center of attention, as he and I were invited to sit at the head table for this gala affair attended by over 1,200 people, including many members of the congressional delegations from a large number of states.

Bill was a loyal and warm friend. Many of his friends I met in Washington were much younger then he and, in *their* loyalty, were almost like members of a Douglas mafia. His term on the Supreme Court was one of the very longest on record. Many conservatives thought it was far too long.

We kept in touch until he had some serious strokes and had to resign from the Court, and, even after that, his fourth wife, whom I had met on a couple of occasions, continued to respond to my letters.

A Gunfighter, a Prince, and a King

Whenever I mention some of the interesting people I've met, the one who seems to draw the most questions is Wyatt Earp, the gunslinger and alleged outlaw of Tombstone fame.

Most people think I'm joking because they have the notion that Wyatt Earp has been dead a hundred years or so. When I tell them that I met him and had lunch with him in 1927 and that he died in 1929, they then begin to ask questions about how I happened to meet him, where we had lunch, and a hundred other things.

In 1927, when I was twenty-one, my father and I went over to the Old Pueblo Club to have lunch. It was a downtown businessmen's club, located on South Stone Avenue in Tucson. Standing on the sidewalk in front of the club was Billy Breckenridge, former U.S. marshal in Tombstone during the time when that town was earning its reputation as being too tough to die. He was a good friend of my father's, and my father introduced me to him. He told us that he was waiting for Wyatt Earp, who should be showing up any minute. He said to my dad, "Since you know him well, why don't you join us for lunch?"

Earp did arrive soon. After proper greetings, I was introduced to him, and we went upstairs to the dining room, where we had lunch. Before Earp had arrived, Billy Breckenridge and my father had agreed that Earp was an outlaw and a killer. He was certainly not the folk hero that he is today. Breckenridge later wrote a book about Tombstone's hectic history in which, I understand, he told it like it was, including some tales about Wyatt Earp and his brother who, at a later time, had been a U.S. marshal assigned to Tombstone.

In answer to questions about the conversation at lunch, I always have to admit that I don't recall any exciting things being discussed. Most of the conversation was about people who were mutual friends from the early days of Tombstone. My dad had been an outstanding baseball player, and Earp and he had become acquainted as a result of the Tucson team's visits to Tombstone.

I don't remember telling anyone about having lunch with Wyatt Earp until many years later, when he began to be looked upon as some kind of hero. That was certainly not his image around Arizona where many people knew and remembered him. I never heard anything from those folks about any of the good or great deeds that he is supposed to have done. He was a tough survivor when some of his close friends and relatives weren't so lucky in avoiding a violent death.

Perhaps my memories of him are tinged by the fact that, when I was a youngster, I met a man who was a real hero to all the kids in our nation and to many adults, also. I'm speaking of William Cody, more popularly known as Buffalo Bill. My brother and I met him when he was in town with the Barnum & Bailey Circus about 1914 and he visited an old friend of his, a Colonel Stevens, who lived two doors from us on South Main Street. I'll never forget his friendly smile and his blue eyes, as well as the long fringe on the sleeves of his leather coat.

In any case, Earp died at home, in bed, in a town in middle California in 1929 at the age of eighty-two. He had been married for many years to a woman he had become acquainted with in Tombstone. She was Jewish, and the two of them are buried in a Jewish cemetery.

To go from one extreme to another, I met the Prince of Wales when he and the woman for whom he relinquished his kingdom visited Tucson back in the late 1950s. He played golf one day at the Tucson Country Club with Erie Ball, the club pro, who was an Englishman by birth and the son of a famous English professional golfer, John Ball.

I was in the foursome playing immediately in back of the prince's group. The play was slow, and we usually reached the tee while they were waiting to tee off. We all met His Royal Highness and visited with him and his group on many of the tees. He was friendly and made a favorable impression on all of us in our foursome. I well remember what a member of the Lewis Douglas family said about the king and the royal family. Douglas, a member of an old Arizona family for whom the town of Douglas, Arizona, is named, had been the U.S. ambassador to England's court of Saint James. The family member, whose name shall not be disclosed, told me that if the male members of the royal family had not been of royal birth, they would have probably been barbers or bartenders.

The Prince and Wally Simpson were guests of the Arizona Inn for a week to ten days. The story went the rounds that this royal party, which consisted of several secretaries and attendants, were truly "guests" of the inn, as they were wherever they stayed. They never paid for their room or meals, it was said. The various resorts and hotels were anxious to have the royal couple stay with them because of their publicity value.

Several Tucsonans at that time thought that the royal party was not entitled to such treatment and criticized them for imposing on the inn, all of which probably would not have bothered the prince and Wally one little bit.

While I was on a People to People golf tour in 1962, I had the pleasure of playing with another ex-king, the deposed Don Juan de Bourbon of Spain, father of Juan Carlos, the present king. We were just south of Lisbon at a famous resort, Estoril. We spent the entire day and evening together, and I found him to be a delightful guy.

As we were walking down the first fairway, I said to him, "Don Juan, you speak perfect English," to which he replied, "Why the hell shouldn't I? Queen Victoria was my grandmother!"

I asked him if he was going to the party that night that was being held for us. He said, "I will unless my old lady wants to stay home." Just like it is in the USA on some occasions. He was a regular guy. That evening while he and I were having a drink in the bar just outside the large dining room, I told him that I had read in the paper that Franco, who then ruled Spain with an iron hand, had been quoted as saying that he might restore Don Juan's son to the throne when he retired, which raised Don Juan's blood pressure a bit because he got right in my face and with his finger pounding on my chest, emphatically told me, "There's one thing Franco forgets. I am the King of Spain and I'll decide who occupies the throne when Franco leaves!" Unfortunately, it didn't work out that way. Don Juan's son was restored to the throne and has been the ruler of Spain since Franco's demise.

Don Juan and I were the last ones in the bar enjoying our conversation. Finally, a friend of his came and told him that all the patrons were standing by their tables waiting for him to enter so they could be seated. He took me by the arm, and he went to the dining room and every one of the 200 people present then sat down. He was very popular with the Portuguese and was treated like royalty of Portugal would have been treated. The dancing commenced after dinner and he danced the first dance with my wife, which was considered to be an honor for her by those present.

I remember at the time shaking my head and wondering if I was dreaming or had I really spent a day with the king of Spain and an evening with the queen whose predecessors some 470 years before were Queen Isabelle and King Ferdinand, about whom I had read of sending Christopher Columbus on his history-making trip across the seas to discover America. It was a long way from 233 South Main Street and those third grade history lessons, but it proves that strange things do indeed happen.

Social Life

Two Hundred Twenty Prostitutes and Three Madams

As I've said, I was born in a large adobe house on the northeast corner of South Main and McCormick Streets. A block and a half east of our house was Tucson's "Red-Light District," known as "Gay Alley." It consisted of two blocks of adobe row housing along Sabino Street. The street dead-ended at McCormick and ran north from there toward Congress.

There were 220 legal prostitutes working in those houses, which were dominated by a two-story house on the south side of McCormick. This larger building was occupied by three madams who could look straight down Gay Alley and see what was going on with the ladies and their clients. I learned later that they controlled that area pretty much with iron fists.

We had to walk right past Gay Alley on our way to and from school. When I was in the fourth grade or so, some city fathers decided that we youngsters should not be exposed to such a dastardly place and erected a corrugated iron fence that had no gates but forced you to walk around it without being able to look straight down Gay Alley. Someone thought that we needed that protection. Whether they were right or wrong, I don't know, but we got it anyway.

Half a block west of Gay Alley, on the corner of Meyer and McCormick, there were two Chinese grocery stores and two saloons. One of the Chinese grocery stores backed up to our backyard.

The neighborhood was not one of the better ones in Tucson. On many occasions, we would hear the loud talking and fighting that would go on outside of the saloons when the customers had become too rowdy to be allowed to remain inside.

I believe the only argument I ever heard my father and mother have was the result of my mother's ardent desire to move out of that area. The home in which my brothers and I were born had been owned by my grandmother, with whom my father lived until he married at the age of thirty-two. My mother finally prevailed, and we moved out of that neighborhood in 1915, when I was nine years old.

I remember that I hated to leave the neighborhood and all my boyhood friends, most of whom were Mexican-American kids with whom I had very close ties. We moved to South Stone Avenue blocks away, which was an entirely different kind of neighborhood.

In 1915, the state of Arizona outlawed prostitution, and most of the ladies who had been making a living on "Gay Alley" disappeared into the community or moved to some other state. However, for many years, illegal houses of prostitution continued to exist in the Tucson area.

In the late 1920s and into the 1930s, one particular woman was well known throughout the community as a madam who ran houses of prostitution at various locations in Tucson. Her name was Mary Branson.

One of her places of business was located in the area north and west of the city hall, a part of town known in those days as Snob Hollow. Many of Tucson's more affluent families lived in large homes there.

It was common knowledge what went on in Mary Branson's two-story house in Snob Hollow. She usually had three or four girls working for her and generally had no problems with the law. Whether the police were being paid off, I don't know, but I am certain that the police felt, as many other men did at the time, that she was providing an important service to the community. Be that as it may.

Mary Branson was a good businesswoman. Everybody in town knew what she did, and she made no bones about it. She contributed to charities and, other than breaking the law by having her business, she was a model citizen.

I remember that one young woman working for her had a daughter who was about thirteen or fourteen years old. The prostitute was usually well dressed and conducted herself very properly. She would meet her daughter in front of Jones Drug on the southwest corner of Scott and Congress. They would go into the drugstore and have a soda.

No doubt, the daughter was receiving money from her mother, and she probably had no idea what her mother did for a living.

An Old Tucson Tradition Sadly Lost

ONE OF THE things I remember as a youngster growing up on South Main Street and McCormick is the musical serenaders who would wake us up in the small hours of the night. They were musicians who worked for my father down at the old Elysian Grove entertainment park, just a block away from our home.

During the summer months, the Grove was a popular gathering place for Tucson residents who attended its plays and musical shows, as well as participated in such things as roller skating, dances, and sometimes even a movie.

My dad often had an orchestra playing at the Grove as part of the entertainment. On many occasions, three or four of the musicians would stop by our home at one or two in the morning and, from the street outside the bedroom window, play some of my mother and father's favorite songs. It was a lovely thing to hear in the middle of the night, those musicians tuning up their fiddles and trumpets and serenading my parents.

In fact, serenading in those days was quite common. It was a tradition that continued for many years, even up until the war days of the 1940s.

There was a favorite Tucson nightspot on South Sixth Avenue then called the La Jolla Club, operated by Jimmie Carter. It was one of the few Tucson nightclubs that boasted an orchestra of live musicians and professional entertainers.

One of the most ardent customers of the La Jolla Club was a man by the name of Len White, who owned a large, successful construction company. He loved to go to the La Jolla Club to drink, eat, and dance. When the evening was over, he would often hire two or three of the musicians to follow him in their car to serenade some friend of his for whom he wanted to do something nice.

The serenaders would drive up alongside the bedroom, if possible, or, if not, get out of their cars and go near the bedroom window and serenade the sleeping friends. The friends were supposed to get up and invite the serenaders in for a drink or two, no matter what the hour.

Len White wasn't the only one who went serenading. As in nearly every community, there were amateur musicians in Tucson who played violins or accordions or guitars. It was common for parties in homes to end up with the partygoers sallying forth on a serenading trip to some of their friends' homes. It was a wonderful Tucson tradition that, for some reason, has disappeared.

SPEAKING OF THE La Jolla Club, I had an interesting experience there with a well-known figure by the name of Alistair Cooke.

During the war, about 1942, Alistair Cooke came to Tucson and called on me at the Tucson Sunshine Climate Club, which I was running at the time. That was a tourist promotion organization, which was boosting Tucson and southern Arizona as vacation spots. He was covering the United States and its war effort for the *London Times* and the *Manchester Guardian.*

We spent about three days together visiting the air bases at Davis-Monthan and Marana, or driving down to Fort Huachuca to look over the Convair plant where they were modifying B-24s and attending meetings of the Red Cross and other organizations.

The first evening he was here, I took him out to the La Jolla Club. He was a very easy fellow to be with and most enjoyable company. He told me that he had been collecting the names of a certain type of bar or club that he called a "joint." Not just every nightclub or bar, he said, qualified for his definition of a joint. In fact, few of them did.

The second night, we went back to the La Jolla Club for dinner. He observed what Jimmie Carter was doing as the proprietor, running the spotlights for the acts, introducing them, dancing with women who might have come in with a group, acting as a peacemaker or bouncer, seating people, and even supervising the kitchen and the food. After watching him for the second night, Cooke said, "You know, Roy, this is a 'joint'—this qualifies. Jimmie Carter makes this place operate as a joint should operate and it fully meets my qualifications!"

When I told Jimmie that later, he laughed and said that he was happy to know that at least somebody appreciated what he was doing.

Fighting and Gambling Times

IN THE DAYS when I was growing into manhood, from around 1915 to 1930, males in Tucson thought and talked more about fistfighting and standing up to protect one's honor than at any other time during my life since, it seems. Of course, now boys and men kill each other over practically nothing instead of becoming involved in a fistfight.

From the time I was six or seven years old, my dad let me know that I was not to back off if some kid did something that I should not accept without physically trying to stop the kid or fighting him. As an example, a boy about my age who lived across the street took something from my younger brother, who came home whimpering that this bigger kid had stolen a spinning top from him. The kid was still in the street playing with other boys. My dad directed me to go and get the top back, even if it meant a fight. I went to the culprit and told him to give me the top. When he refused, we squared off and went at it. He went home crying, and I got the top back.

Another time my dad noticed that the pocket on my shirt was partially torn. He asked me what happened. When I told him a boy had torn it as I was coming home from school, he asked me what I did to the boy about it. I said I hadn't done anything because I had been given a brand-new geography book as an award for a good grade and didn't want to lay it down on the dirt to fight. He said that was no excuse; he told me to go and send the kid home crying. I had to go back, find the kid, and let him know that he shouldn't have picked on me.

I had a lot of those fistfights, as most kids did. It was common to see fights on or just off the school grounds. Kids often recounted particularly good fights they were involved in or had seen. My dad bought two pair of boxing gloves for my brother Frank and me, and we had many sparring matches—none when we were mad at each other but often when we had nothing better to do. It was good training.

I recall one particular fight I had while I was in high school. It was with a black kid, the first of three allowed to go to Tucson High School, and it occurred just as school was letting out. We fought on the athletic field across from the school and attracted a crowd of a couple of hundred students. No one suffered serious damage, and I know that both he and I were happy when some guys stepped in and stopped us.

The boy was Rufus Flewellen, with whom I later established a good friendship that endured for many years after school days. He was a Pullman porter working out of San Francisco. So fighting was common enough that enemies did not remain enemies for long. I even had fights after I was married and running the theaters, some during ball games in which I was either playing or managing a team.

I hope I don't give you the impression that I was a combative sort of guy, but usually a fight seemed justified, especially when someone called you an S.O.B. In those days, those were fighting words and justified squaring off.

My dad was known as a battler when he was playing baseball, which he did until about the time he reached forty, either as a player or a manager. One old-timer by the name of Tax Shelton told me several times, always when he was a little drunk, about a famous fight my dad had with a big-league ballplayer who was playing in the winter for a team from Cananea, Mexico, against the Tucson town team. Others, too, told me about fights Dad had during baseball games. So I grew up in the kind of atmosphere in which fistfighting was generally accepted as a way of life.

I remember that on many occasions, when men older than me by a generation, gathered in the Damskey Cigar Store next door to the Opera House on Congress Street, to shoot the bull and discuss local politics. Often the conversation would be about physical prowess and fighting. One local "strong boy" by the name of Duke Snyder (no, not the ballplayer) was especially interested in the subject of fighting. He said to remember that a "good big man can whip a good little man anytime." He thought that was important, for some unknown reason.

DURING THOSE TIMES there were boxing matches every week or so, generally promoted by a man by the name of Louie Gherna. Cockfights, although outlawed, were popular with the gambling crowd. They always somehow found the matches, which were held in secret spots on the west side of town.

There also was a gambling joint, generally operated by a Chinese family, in an old adobe building not too far from where the red-light district had been located before it was outlawed in 1915. I was in it two or three times with cousin Oliver Drachman who liked to shoot craps (which was also illegal). Other kinds of gambling often went on in the back of a cigar store run by Jimmie Rand on Congress, right next to Litt's drugstore, which was on the corner of Stone and Congress.

Jimmie's place was tiny but very busy. Foot traffic on Congress was heavy, and Jimmie did a good business in newspapers, magazines, smokes, and a few other things such as a baseball pool, whose participants would pick a National League team and an American League team and bet on the innings in which the two teams would score the most runs. Tickets sold for fifty cents, and you could buy as many tickets as you wished. The daily pots would run up to $150 or $200 a day and would create a lot of excitement. Jimmie took a fee off the top. The police knew about the pool but allowed it to operate because everyone played and it kept people from going nuts during the hot summers before there was air-conditioning.

Jimmie also had "punch boards." They were generally against the law, too, but difficult to regulate. Jimmie also had football pools, which, again, were illegal but not rigidly pursued by the police.

In the back of Jimmie's, up on a mezzanine with a ceiling so low a man couldn't stand upright beneath it, a poker table was busy most afternoons and evenings with a game that attracted many but could only seat about eight men. Sizable amounts were won and lost among the players, all of whom were downtown businessmen. The place was often crowded with guys who didn't mind the smoke, the poor air circulation, the bad lighting, and the inability to stand erect.

Many men found relaxation at the Old Pueblo Club, the Elk's Club, and others, where such games as *panguinque* (known as "pan" and pronounced "pangingee" by old-timers) were very popular. Those old-timers played it by the hour, using several decks of cards, in a perpetually running game at the Old Pueblo Club. Unfortunately, the Old Pueblo Club, after a run of almost eighty years, no longer exists.

Early Tucson Telephones

I WASN'T AROUND when the first telephones appeared on the scene in the Old Pueblo, but I well remember when, in about 1915, they were still considered to be an unnecessary evil by many people.

As in all places that had phones in those days, they were attached to the wall and consisted of a little box with a bell on the top and a cradle on the side where the receiver hung. The receiver itself was a nearly conical black instrument about six or seven inches long with a round dishlike disk on its large end that you would hold up to your ear. It was connected to the box on the wall by a short, wire cord.

The box also had a mouthpiece sprouting from it into which you'd speak. If you wanted to make a call you would take the receiver off the hook and wait for the operator to ask, "Number please," then give her the number you were calling. She would do the connecting for you.

Often she would be very busy, and you'd have to wait and wait and wait for her to pick up your line. This would infuriate people at times and cause them to give the operator a piece of their mind, which in turn could cause the operator to get even by delaying the ring on the other line or responding with a few choice words of her own.

I had a crotchety old uncle, in fact, who had a reputation for telling people off, particularly those who could not respond promptly. A few times I was present when he tried to make a call, and the operator was a bit slow in asking for the number he was calling. He didn't hesitate to tell her off in a most ungentlemanly—and embarrassing—way. You could be sure that the service on that phone would not be the best for a while.

Generally, though, the service was pretty good. Those who used the phone a lot would sometimes develop a friendly relationship with an operator, who would recognize their voice. I remember that this happened for me with a long-distance operator who would recognize my voice and mention my name. I always got excellent service when she picked up one of my calls. After a number of years, one of those friendly operators finally introduced herself to me, but it was indeed rare that you ever knew what the woman on the other end of the line looked like.

I remember one time in 1933, not too long before my father died, he had some kind of an attack late in the night. I got on the phone and tried unsuccessfully to reach his doctor. When he did not respond, I called another doctor, who also couldn't be reached. I then tried a third doctor with the same results.

When no one answered for the third doctor, the operator came on the line and said, "Mr. Drachman I know you've been trying to reach a doctor without success. I know a doctor who's available." She gave me his name and asked if I wanted her to ring him, which, of course, I did. He came to the house and saw my father.

How the operator knew my name is still a mystery to me, but I do know she was a smart, kind lady who went out of her way to help someone. That was one of the advantages of living in a small Tucson and knowing someone who cared.

Another advantage of living where there were not too many phones was the kind of number you could have. As an example, Monte Mansfeld, who was considered our number one citizen, had a very simple number. If you wanted to call Monte you'd ask the operator just to ring number 1—his office number.

The Old Pueblo Club's number was 10. We all had business numbers with only three digits. The number for the Opera House was 517; for the Rialto Theater it was 903. The number for the *Star* reached an astronomical 2400.

I used the phone a great deal when I was manager of the Tucson Sunshine Climate Club. I had a good memory in those days and kept the numbers of most businesspeople I called in my head. Using the phone book would have been an unnecessary bother.

One time when I introduced the manager of the phone company as the speaker at the Rotary Club, I requested about fifty members of the club to stand. I asked the manager if he knew so-and-so's number, which, in nearly all cases, he didn't. Then I told him what the phone number was for every one of the men, without referring to notes. It was fun and easy only because the numbers were mostly three digits long, of course. After finishing my trick I told the speaker that one of the problems with our phone service resulted from his not knowing the numbers of his customers.

I well remember when the telephone office serving the downtown area consisted of a two-story frame tower on North Grand Avenue. Long after it was abandoned by the phone company, it continued to stand. It should have been saved as a historic building.

When even four-digit numbers reached their maximum capacity, the phone company logically established five-digit ones, and we town boosters felt that Tucson had moved up a notch into big-city status, though in truth Tucson was very much a Johnny-come-lately to such status.

The United States for a great many years has had the best phone service in the world. I know from my own experience how bad the phone service has traditionally been in Mexico, France, Japan, Germany, and even England. I didn't own any phone company stock when that judge decided it should be split up, but I know he didn't do our nation a favor—the result has been a decline in service, confusion for the customers, and no noticeable savings in the cost of using phones.

Screen Porches in Early Tucson

DURING A RECENT very cold spell, I was telling some of my grandchildren that for the first twenty years of my life, I never slept inside but always on a screened-in porch, no matter how cold it got, how much it rained, or how much the wind blew. I told them that most kids in my generation in Tucson did the same. As I mentioned earlier in this book, we had canvas curtains we could tie down to prevent the rain from blowing in on us, but it got pretty darn cold during a typical Tucson winter. That certainly didn't hurt us much, though. Most of us folks lived into our eighties.

When I got married in the winter of 1927, I began sleeping inside for the first time. But that next summer we moved our beds back to the screen porch, which every home in Tucson had at that time. Sleeping was difficult because of the miserable heat. We tried sleeping on cots in the backyard, but that was tough also because of bugs, early daylight, frequent dust storms, and sometimes rain. We used to put sheets in the shower to get them cool to sleep on and when they got dry we'd soak them again. But nothing really worked.

So I decided to move to California. I wasn't going to spend the rest of my life in Tucson's unbearable heat. A friend of mine in the theater business in Los Angeles, Milt Arthur, and I formed a partnership to buy the Belmont Shores Theater near Long Beach. We had an option on it, and I had arranged for my share of the financing.

Shortly after I returned from my trip to the Coast, another friend of mine, Fred Blanc, called one morning and asked me to come down to the sidewalk where he would pick me up to take me to his house to show me something. At his home, he took me to his bedroom, which was blessedly cool. He showed me the first swamp cooler I had ever seen or even heard about. He had built it himself. He had rigged a sixteen-inch electric fan to suck air through a damp pad of excelsior over which water was dripping from his garden hose.

To make a long story short, before the day was over I had built two of them, one for our bedroom window and the other for the living room. I called Milt Arthur a few days later and told him I could now sleep at night and was staying in Tucson.

With the development of air-conditioning that almost every family could afford, major changes occurred in plans for homes built in desert areas. No longer were screen porches included in them. Furthermore, families enclosed their existing screen porches, and converted them to bedrooms or family rooms with air-conditioning.

Tucson High School

CONTRARY TO THE belief some may hold, student strikes in Tucson go back far before the 1960s. There was one at Tucson High, the community's only high school then, on November 11, 1919, which was the first anniversary of the armistice that ended World War I.

The students thought that the occasion warranted a holiday, but the school administration thought otherwise. The president of the student body, Fenimore Cooper, was an excellent speaker and led the movement to declaring the day a special holiday by first appealing to the principal of Tucson High and, when that effort failed, declaring a strike for the next day, Armistice Day.

He called for a rally of the student body on the grounds across the street from the school, which at that time occupied the south wing of the Roskruge School on East Sixth Street. Instead of entering the school building that morning, most of the kids assembled around the back of a small truck that some student drove onto the grounds to serve as a platform for the leaders of the strike.

The newspapers recognized the strike as an important news story and gave it plenty of attention. Fenimore Cooper was quoted as telling his student body, "Follow me and I'll lead you to hell and back again. All the war veterans support our effort to have this day declared a holiday by the school system, as it has been by the city and state. Stick together and we'll beat the school officials."

Other student body officers also spoke, including the secretary of the Tucson High student body, my cousin, Oliver Drachman, whose father, Mose, was a member of the three-man school board. The newspapers made a note of that fact.

The students made their point, didn't attend school that day, and were not penalized for their absence. The next year, when I was a student at Tucson High, it was a school holiday as it was for banks, governmental offices, and all other schools. It still is, though it's now known, of course, as Veterans Day.

Another event that took place about that time involving Tucson High became a real donnybrook for the entire city. It all started in 1920 when I was a freshman. We freshmen had to sit in the balcony

Left to right Roy, Alice, and Oliver Drachman, 1980.

of the school auditorium while Dr. C. E. Rose, superintendent of the Tucson school system, addressed our student body about the importance of the upcoming bond election for the approval of the then large amount of $750,000 for the construction of a new high school building.

Dr. Rose said, "You freshmen sitting up there in the balcony will benefit the most because you will have at least two years to enjoy the new school building." He urged us to tell our parents and others how badly the new building was needed and to get them to go to the polls and vote in favor of the bonds.

The bonds were approved, but that was where the real battle began. Up until that time there had been no mention of the location of the gigantic new high school; most people seemed to assume it would be near the existing high school on East Sixth Street and Second and Third Avenues. However, some powerful people in the city realized the importance of having a new high school on or near their property. It would be a real financial bonanza and could increase the value of their property several times over.

At that time the Steinfeld family was probably the wealthiest group in the city. They owned several blocks of vacant land in the northwest part of town, starting at the northwest corner of Speedway and Stone Avenue and extending to Drachman Street on the north and to Main Street on the west. They proposed that the new high school be built on a block of property near the center of their land. They were successful in calling for an election by taxpayers to determine whether the new school would be located where the school board wanted to put it or where the Steinfeld group wanted it. I should point out that there were many other people who owned land in the northwestern part of town, and they formed a formidable opposition force. As the election date approached, a considerable amount of money was spent on newspaper ads and posters around town, urging the voters to support one location or the other. It was one of the earliest issues to divide the community, and there were some deep feelings among the old-timers in support of their chosen side. The scars from that election did not go away rapidly.

The Steinfeld interests, which included many besides that family, did not carry the day, and the school was constructed at its present site. The battle over the location delayed construction for several months, so those of us freshmen sitting in the balcony the day Dr. Rose asked for our support never did get to attend the new school. Its first graduating class was that of 1925. We had to have our graduation exercises in the auditorium of the old Safford School on South Fifth Avenue. The 142 members of our graduating class of 1924 and their families filled that facility that evening.

As I noted a bit earlier, Tucson High School didn't have any black students until about 1922, when three students were allowed to register and attend classes. The three students were Teddy Preston, Rufus Flewellen, and his sister, whose name I can't recall. They'd attended Paul Lawrence Dunbar School on West Second Street, which was a combination elementary and middle school for blacks only. This was before the Tucson Schools were integrated, of course; unfortunately it was many years before that occurred.

The U of A Back When

IN 1924 WHEN I registered at the University of Arizona as a freshman, the hazing of first-year students was commonplace. This included paddling freshmen for infractions of various kinds of silly rules. For example, from the beginning of the school year until well into the spring semester we were required to wear green beanie caps outdoors at all times. If we were caught without our beanie, we'd get a paddling in front of the Agricultural Building, which was the heart of the campus.

It was customary to have a daily gathering of students in front of the "Aggy" building, where there was a large bulletin board on which the names of those people to be punished that afternoon would be posted. A Traditions Committee, made up largely of upper classmen, both established and enforced the rules. Paddling was the principal punishment, but there were other things a guilty freshman would be required to do such as scrubbing the cement plaza in front of the Aggy building on his hands and knees. Paddling was done by upper classmen using three-foot-long, heavy wooden paddles, which caused painful, but not dangerous, suffering.

There were great competitive feelings between the freshman and sophomore classes, which resulted in the sophomores spying on and attempting to catch freshmen breaking the rules. Soon after the start of the second semester, a basketball game was always scheduled between the freshman and sophomore teams. If the freshmen won, they could discontinue wearing the green beanies about a month earlier than was normally allowed. The game was scheduled to be played in the gym located in the tiny Herring Hall.

The balcony above the court at the west end of the gym was very small, with room for an audience of only about sixty or seventy people. I remember that our freshman team was badly beating the sophomores when, near the end of the game, one of the sophomore players threw the ball up into the balcony. A small group of sophomores caught the ball and promptly punctured it with a pocket knife. That ended the game, because no other ball was available. The game was postponed for a few weeks and our team won, so we were allowed to remove our beanies early.

One of the things freshmen had to endure from sophomores was being picked up when they were caught alone at night, taken out eight or ten miles into the desert, and dumped. The walk home was a tough ordeal on a dark, cold night. We finally organized and would walk to town to a movie or to go to Dooley's to play pool in small groups. We also began to be more aggressive, taking sophomores for rides into the desert.

During that time, the men on campus became annoyed that the popular girls in the various sorority houses were making dates two and three weeks in advance. The guys weren't used to that kind of treatment—they expected to make a date no more than a few days in advance. So they organized a revolt and formed the "Bachelors' Club," which established a month-long boycott of the girls in the four or five houses where most of the very popular girls lived. Tucson girls were also included in the boycott, and this led to an "incident" in which one of the guys who had signed up as a member of the Bachelors' Club was caught by snooping bachelors, who peaked through a window of the home of a local girl and found him in her living room. He was censured and fined.

All this now seems to be much ado about nothing, but it was considered important at the time to the boys who were trying to assert themselves.

Another bit of foolishness in those days created much glee and excitement and caused embarrassment for a new smart aleck on the campus. Some guy who had been acting obnoxiously for one reason or another became the object of a trick that usually became a very hilarious event.

A "badger fight" would be announced for a certain afternoon in front of the Aggy building. The event was to be a fight between a wild, ferocious badger and a bulldog. The badger was supposedly to be kept under a wooden box. The bulldog would be held on a leash, waiting for the badger to be pulled from under the box by a rope around its neck. It was stressed that it was an honor to be chosen to pull the badger from under the box to face the bulldog.

The badger fight was well advertised by posters and an announcement on the campus bulletin board. The smart aleck was given the "honor" of pulling the badger from under the box, which would be lifted to release it. Usually a crowd of several hundred excited students would be on hand to witness the historic fight.

There was only one thing wrong with the event. Instead of the rope's being attached to a badger, it was tied to a piss pot, which the honoree dragged behind him as he followed his instructions to run like hell when he pulled the badger from under its wooden cage. Usually someone would have a camera handy to record the event at its peak. The stigma of being the butt of the trick usually brought the honoree down off his high horse and provided a lot of fun—for all but one person.

During the last years of the 1920s, the university produced an exceptional musical show that featured original musical numbers starring girls and guys of the student body. The show was called the Senior Follies and was presented at the downtown Rialto Theater at reserved seat performances for two or three nights. George Whettle, an older student who had been through the First World War and who later had a career in the theater business, was the producer and also the composer of much of the original music. He collaborated with Gene Quaw, a professional musician who played in a musical group at the Rialto and composer of several musical numbers, including the well-known "Kitten on the Keys."

The sets and drapes as well as the costumes were designed and created by the Art department. The show was very popular for the three or four years it was presented. It was a sellout at the box office and was really a thoroughly professional production. Some of the stars were Dottie Coburn, Alice West Drachman, Bill Berry, Bill Carraway—who did a song and dance number—and many other talented kids. The chorus line featured many girls from the campus. Its numbers always brought down the house.

In those days there were only 1,300 to 1,500 students registered at the University. All of us knew everyone else on campus, making it great fun to attend the University of Arizona.

Agnes Parties

ONE OF THE highlights of the beginning of every school year at the University of Arizona was the "Agnes Parties." They were a great deal of fun for the older students, but a great embarrassment to some newcomer who thought he was a great lover.

These Agnes Parties were not exclusively collegiate and were often staged by some of the older guys in order to liven up a dull summer when the "summer bachelors," whose families had gone away to cooler climes, had nothing better to do than to pull a trick on some innocent friend.

I was involved in quite a few Agnes Parties, as were many other fellows during those days when the Depression made a watermelon bust a big deal. No one had any money, and we had to amuse ourselves some way.

I remember one Agnes Party in particular.

A man by the name of Burt Jones had been transferred to Tucson to manage the Lyric Theater. At the time, I was managing the Fox

Theater. Both theaters were owned by the Fox West Coast Theater Company.

Burt was a handsome guy and a beautiful dresser, and he bragged occasionally about some of his romantic conquests. However, he was so busy working at the theater, attempting to turn it from a loser to a winner, he really hadn't had time to get acquainted with any local ladies.

My cousin Oliver and I decided that he would be a great victim for an Agnes Party. Oliver started telling him about a very beautiful woman he knew and whom Burt would probably like. However, Oliver told him that he wasn't going to introduce him to this lady because her husband was a friend, and he didn't want to be involved in helping her cheat on her husband.

Of course, this was totally fictitious.

A couple of weeks later, I told Burt, "You know, I can tell you who Agnes is. I remember meeting her. She is a gorgeous. Her husband is a railroad man, gone a great deal of the time, and is an alcoholic." I said that I understood that he was cheating on his wife when he would go out of town on his trips.

When we had Burt well set up for this lady, finally I told him that I had worked it out so that I would take him to her house and introduce him. Then he could spend the evening with her.

As he told the story later, he went to the barber and got a haircut, was properly perfumed, and had even pressed his shoelaces so that he would make a proper impression on Agnes.

We used the home of a man whose family was out of town and, of course, the party wasn't a party unless you had a good number of people involved in it. It wasn't difficult to gather a few friends at someone's home in anticipation of an Agnes Party.

On this particular night, Burt came to the Fox after hours and he and I took off to see Agnes. I had told him that she liked watermelon and that he should bring a big one along to present to her. This, of course, was going to be a treat for the rest of us afterward.

We parked in front of the house, which was on a dark street. At the front door, I softly said, "Agnes, Agnes, can we come in?"

With that, a man burst out of the door with a gun in his hand, yelling, "I'll Agnes you, you no good S.O.B. You're the guy that's been fooling around with my wife!" Then he fired a couple of shots, which, of course, were blanks. I fell down on the edge of the lawn and told Burt to run for his life, that this man was going to kill us both.

However, I've got to tell the truth about Burt Jones. He didn't run. He said that he could not leave his friend dying on this lawn. At that, the irate "husband" shouted, "Get the son of a bitch off my lawn. I don't want him to die on my property."

By that time, I was beginning to break up. The lights flashed on inside the house, and everyone came pouring out the door, laughing and looking to see what had happened to the victim.

He was standing alongside me on the lawn, and when he realized that it was all a hoax, he joined in the laughter and enjoyed the drinks and watermelon served to the witnesses of this "shooting."

Agnes Parties went on for years around Tucson and I'm not sure that it still doesn't go on, under one name or another.

I remember one particular case when we pulled such a trick on someone, who outsmarted us.

A traveling man with one of the Vaudeville acts that used to come through Tucson quite regularly indicated that he would like to meet a nice lady and spend an evening with her. I couldn't resist the opportunity to have another Agnes Party.

My parents were out of town at the time, so we decided to use their home. I had arranged to have about a dozen guys show up. We bought a hundred bottles of "home brew" from a brew master by the name of Post and put it and a hundred pounds of ice in the bathtub.

We delegated a man with a booming voice to play the role of the husband and to do the shooting. Everything was set and went well until I walked up to the house with the Vaudevillian in the dark night and softly called for Agnes. After a couple of minutes, the man with the booming voice opened the door and said, "I'll Agnes you, you S.O.B. You've been fooling around with my wife and I'm going to kill you!"

With that he fired a couple of blanks and I yelled to my friend that he should run, that I was shot, and that he would kill him, too.

The victim, instead of running, pulled out a revolver, pushed it through the screen door, and smashed the glass in the front door. Then he opened fire into the living room.

At that turn of events, I was pleading with him to stop shooting. I said that this was all a joke, that we were having fun, and that he should please not take it seriously. To this he said, "I'm going around the backdoor and I'm going to clean out this joint. I'll show this guy how to handle a gun."

Eventually, I prevailed, after hanging on his arm and pleading with him to cool down. The lights came on in the house, and everyone was seriously shaken and wondering if anybody had been hit.

We found out later that my father's partner, Ben Goldsmith, had tipped off this stranger and told him what was going to happen. They decided to reverse the roles of the sucker and the smart guy and bought a bunch of blanks for his revolver, which he used to scare the hell out of us that night.

It was a good lesson and, from then on, we were very cautious about identifying the victim and being certain that he was not tipped off in advance.

An Unusual and Humorous Fishing Trip

As THE COUNTRY was coming out of the Depression in the 1930s, it was common for Tucson families to drive up to the White Mountains for weekends to fish and to get out of the heat. We had done so several times with our youngsters and had a lot of fun.

So we decided we would join three other couples and go up for a long weekend at a lodge near Alpine, Arizona. Those three couples were Mr. and Mrs. Harold Tovrea, Dr. and Mrs. Holly Trimble, and Mike and Helen Casteel. (Mike was the football coach at the University of Arizona at the time.)

The Trimbles and Tovreas went ahead in one car, and we and the Casteels followed them in another. It was agreed that we would stop wherever they did. Because Trimble had made the trip a number of times, he knew where every bar was along the way. We stopped four or five times and had a "nip," or a cold drink for those ladies who were driving. It took us most of the day to get up there, but we had a lot of laughs along the way.

During the first morning, we men got up early to go fishing. Trimble was somewhat lame and couldn't walk very well, so he decided that he would bring along a book to read and a bottle, which would come in handy, naturally, in case someone was bitten by a snake. He never got more than fifty feet from the car while the three of us walked up and down the streams supposedly catching fish for our dinner.

We ate dinner at the lodge that evening.

The next day, we headed for the Blue River, which was along the eastern boundary of Arizona. Friends of ours, Mr. and Mrs. Don Fogg, had a summer home on the river and had invited us to come over, spend the day with them, and fish the streams in that area.

We men went fishing while the ladies stayed with the Foggs, having lunch and doing a little drinking themselves. When we got back at about five or six, one of the ladies, Helen Casteel, had "taken on quite a load" and was feeling no pain. Someone suggested that we take her down to the stream and have her put her feet in the water, which would help to sober her up before the bumpy drive back to our lodge. The stream was a puny one, only about eight feet wide, and could be crossed by stepping on a couple of rocks. It was never deeper than three or four inches, but it would serve Helen's needs well.

The Foggs had set up a white tent between their home and the stream for their children to sleep in when they came up from Tucson. Just as we got down to the water, Helen suddenly looked up and saw it. "My God," she shouted. "We've got to get out of here! Here comes a sailboat!" To a person, we all collapsed in hysterics. Even a kid's sailboat couldn't float in that stream!

The next day, we went fishing again, but Trimble stayed at the lodge with the ladies, playing pitch. We got back about midafternoon, told Trimble that the fish were biting and that we'd had a great day. Not to be outdone, he decided that he would take a line down to a small wooden bridge over the stream nearby and try to catch a fish or two.

No fly fisherman, he took a can of worms with him and was getting ready to put a line in the water when he suddenly yelled. He had stuck the hook in his thumb beyond the barb and couldn't get it out. He stumbled back up to the lodge where we were sitting and, thinking he was overdoing it, laughing at him. Mike Casteel said that the worm had outfought him and had forced the hook into him, rather than vice versa.

It turned out, however, that Trimble was indeed in trouble and was in considerable pain. The operators of the lodge told us that there was one of Roosevelt's Civilian Conservation Corps camps down the road about five miles, where there was a doctor. Trimble took a big snort of whiskey, and we drove to the CCC camp. The elderly doctor who was taking care of the 250 or so young men doing all kinds of community work in the area—building bridges and fences, improving the highway, and so on—agreed to help.

The doctor took one look at Trimble's thumb and said that he would have to push the hook through beyond the barb then cut the barb off and remove the hook. He told Trimble that it would be very painful. He asked his young orderly to bring over a bottle of whiskey from a nearby shelf and a glass. When Trimble heard that, his eyes began to roll and he cleared his throat, sure he was going to get another snort.

However, he was in for a surprise. The doctor poured about two ounces of whiskey in the glass, raised it to his lips and drank it down. Then, braced for action, he pushed the hook through Trimble's thumb, cut off the barb and removed the hook.

We men were in hysterics again—except for poor Trimble, whose face showed as much disappointment as pain.

On Sunday, the lady at the lodge told her husband to go out and kill two or three chickens for a fried chicken dinner she had been promising for several days. She had a good-sized chicken pen out in the backyard, and her husband, who was well inebriated at the time, went out (not very happily) to do her bidding. Apparently he had his own idea of just how to go about that chore, because, all of a sudden, we heard an earsplitting volley of gunshots and we all rushed to see what was wrong.

Well, that was the first and last time I ever saw anyone trying to kill a chicken with a six-shooter. Slugs were ricocheting off the rocks, wreaking havoc in all directions. They were sending stones zinging everywhere and whining as they cut through the air. When the gunslinger's wife could make herself heard over the commotion, she ordered him to put the gun away and to kill the chickens with a more traditional method.

He wasn't pleased with the suggestion and refused to kill the chickens. She asked if any of us fellows had ever killed chickens and I told her that I had cut off the heads of many victims when I was a young man, visiting my grandfather in Huntington Beach, California.

She told me, "There's a hatchet in the back. Pick out three good chickens and cut off their heads and we'll have them for lunch."

I followed directions, killed the chickens, and, after they were through flopping around, brought them in, where she plucked the feathers and prepared a nice luncheon for us.

That was the best fishing trip I ever went on.

Place and Places

Tucson in the Teens

BACK IN TUCSON'S second decade in this century, from 1910 to 1920, one of the town's important events was the Pima County Fair. The Fair was held at the fairgrounds, which, at that time, were east of the extended line of South Campbell Avenue and south of the Southern Pacific railroad tracks. East Thirty-Sixth Street, as it is now located, would have run pretty close to the southern boundary of the fairgrounds.

I believe that the property was owned by the Albert Steinfeld family and was managed by Al Donau, a Steinfeld in-law. It contained a farming operation of only modest size but did include quite a few fruit trees such as figs, peaches, and apples, as well as a number of olive trees.

Probably its most important feature was an oval auto racetrack about a mile long. Local auto buffs raced against each other on it and sometimes against entries from Phoenix and El Paso. Once in a while, some internationally known race drivers would come to town and race for cash prizes.

I remember the first auto race I ever saw was at that track and starred two world-famous drivers: Barney Oldfield and Ralph De-Palma. They brought to town the latest models of racing automobiles, which were often two-seaters, with the nondriving member of the team being responsible for hand-operating a pump that was somehow connected to the flow of the gasoline tank to the engine. The drivers would usually wear some kind of silk scarf, which would be flying in the air as they sped around the oval track.

Barney Oldfield was known for always having a cigar in his mouth as he drove and when he lit the cigar, it was a signal that he was going to win the race and that the fat lady could start singing.

Although there weren't many automobiles on the streets, there was a great fascination among the general public about the autos and their ability to go "lickety split" at sixty miles an hour! There were often arguments among the fans about the ability of a person to breathe in an open car going at that speed. The track was banked at the curves and was often sprinklered to reduce the dust from the speeding autos.

For several years during that period, there was an annual El Paso to Phoenix Road Race, which attracted drivers from all over the country and which featured race drivers from cities in Texas, New Mexico, and Arizona. I remember that Tucson's favorite son, Dick Clark, would have an entry that he drove in the race. In fact, he was credited with having built the racer in his garage here in Tucson.

The cars would turn north on South Sixth Avenue off the El Paso Road and then swing northwest at Seventeenth Street onto South Stone Avenue, right through the heart of Tucson's downtown and on to the road to Florence. The race would start early in the morning in El Paso, with the racers hitting Tucson sometime around midday. People would be lined up along Stone Avenue waiting to watch the speed demons go by. It created great excitement, especially among us kids.

ANOTHER IMPORTANT PLACE in Tucson in those days was the Elysian Grove, an amusement park owned by my father, Emanuel Drachman, and Nat Hawke. The town baseball park was located there. That was when baseball was the most important game in town. The wooden grandstand would hold about a thousand people with bleachers providing seats for another five hundred fans.

The Elysian Grove was on South Main Street where the Carrillo School is now located. It included thirteen acres of land on which several hundred umbrella and ash trees provided shaded areas for picnic tables. Tucson's first swimming pool was in the Grove, as was the Pavilion, a large wooden structure built like a Quonset hut. It had a hardwood floor and was used for dances and as a skating rink with a large mechanical music box providing bandlike music for dancers and skaters.

Left to right Albert, Roy, mother, Millie, and Frank Drachman, about 1936.

The Grove also had an outdoor beer garden and saloon, which were well patronized before or after ball games and parties in the pavilion. An airdrome, which was an outdoor theater where Arizona's first motion pictures were shown and where stage shows were regularly presented during the summer months, contained bench seats for about 500 people. That was where my mother, Millie Royers, first appeared as a singer booked out of Los Angeles. Following her second summer appearance, she and my father were married.

The city limits on the north end of Tucson stopped then at the corner of North Stone Avenue and Speedway. One Fourth of July, my Uncle Herb Drachman had brought back from a trip to San Francisco a large collection of fireworks that couldn't legally be set off inside the city limits. So we gathered at Mulberry Park, located at Stone and Speedway, and watched Uncle Herb shoot off the several boxes of fireworks on the north side of Speedway, just across the street from the city limits.

There wasn't a thing on the horizon north of Speedway clear to the Catalina Mountains and there wasn't much development west or northwest of the Stone and Speedway intersection.

I well remember when East Sixth Street ended at Campbell Avenue. A barbed wire fence ran along the east side of Campbell and from there, you had a clear view of the Rincon Mountains. There were very few houses between that point and them. Shortly after 1920, a real estate developer by the name of A. I. Winsett acquired an eighty-acre parcel of land there and created a subdivision, with East Sixth Street as the principal street between Campbell and Tucson Boulevard.

Winsett paved Sixth Street and all the cross streets north to Fifth Street and south to Eighth Street. He sold lots both to home builders and to individuals. As new families moved into Tucson, this new subdivision became a popular residential area. And as permanent Tucson residents recognized the advantages of the new eastside locations, it wasn't long before other large subdivisions, such as El Encanto and Colonia Solana, were developed and became home for many prominent Tucson families.

Mountains and Streams around Tucson

MOUNTAINS WE HAVE plenty. Streams we have few.

When we were kids, my brother and I did a lot of exploring. Our house on South Main Street was about a block north of the present Carrillo School and about a half block north of where the El Minuto Mexican restaurant is. Across the street from our house ran a row of adobe homes. Immediately in back of those houses to the west were the *milpas* (farm fields) through which we hiked many times on our way to the Santa Cruz River, in the bed of which a small stream usually trickled. Just beyond the river were the adobe ruins of an old church that is considered quite historic today. A short distance west of the old ruins and beyond a small field, a cement irrigation ditch flowed north. There were pumping stations all along the ditch, which was about eight feet wide at the ground level and five feet wide at its bottom. The water in it was about three feet deep and flowed fairly fast, which made it attractive for a dip, though signs warned against it.

Near the ditch were the ruins of Warner's Mill, which originally had been powered by a sluice carrying water from the Santa Cruz. The mill was built of fieldstone found in the area and stood for many, many years after it ceased to operate, which was long before my time.

Just west of the ditch was Mission Road, a winding dirt thoroughfare running right next to the foot of Sentinel Peak, more commonly known now as A Mountain. We boys used to roam often all over that area. Many times we climbed Sentinel Peak, long before the A was constructed. Although a dirt road ran up to the top about where the present road is located, we never used it.

For a while we were hesitant to explore the large hill to the northwest known as Tumamoc Hill, where later a University of Arizona research institute was established. Then, when we first reached the top of it, we were surprised to see that it was much higher than Sentinel Peak, had a much larger area, and had been, no doubt, inhabited by early Indian tribes—we found hollowed-out places in large flat rocks where they had ground corn.

We seldom encountered any other people roaming these mountains and, in fact, often skinny-dipped in the irrigation ditch during the summer months.

It wasn't much of a hike from our house across the fields and through the Santa Cruz to the ditch and up the mountain. But as we grew a little older, though still under ten, we ventured far to the east beyond the university, which was considered "way out." We twice hiked from our Main Street home to Ft. Lowell, some seven miles away. For lunch, we carried a canteen of water and a couple of hot dogs and rolls. We knew there was a stream about three or four feet wide called, I believe, the Romero Ditch, that ran in that area, and which came from a spring to the east, about where the Tucson Country Club is now. So we brought along a pot in which we would cook the hot dogs. After exploring the region near the old abandoned fort, we would hike back home, which was a good day's trip for a couple of youngsters

When we joined the Boy Scouts a few years later, we went on a camping trip to Sabino Canyon, which, of course, had a pretty good stream of water that ran year-round. Just a quarter of a mile from where the road ended at the mouth of Sabino, located right next to a rather steep rock embankment, there was a pond we called Sandy Hole because it had a sand bottom. It was about ten feet deep and a great swimming hole, the only one in the canyon for a mile or so. We used to swim there au natural, even on Sundays, knowing no one would see us. We went there many times and thought it to be a heavenly place, which it still is.

The first real summer camp the Boy Scouts held was a two-week outing at Gardner Canyon on the eastern slope of the Santa Rita Mountains, some forty miles south of Tucson near Mt. Whetstone, better known as Old Baldy. There was a small stream running at that time in Gardner Canyon, although we camped near the old ranch house and its more dependable supply of well water.

For many of us, the trip was our first one away from Mama and Papa, and we had great fun. We played baseball daily, when we weren't involved in learning things Boy Scouts were supposed to know from our scout leader, Newsome Housewald.

The highlight of that camping trip was an overnight hike up an eight-mile trail to the top of Mt. Baldy, which is 9,432 feet high. We could see nearly all of southern Arizona from there, and even the Sea of Cortez, known to gringos as the Gulf of California.

The highest 500 feet of that peak are above the timber line and indeed bald. On the very top, there was a lookout tower from which a forest ranger could survey the entire mountain range. A telephone line was his only connection to the world.

About a half mile from the tower stood a small cabin where the ranger lived. By the time we reached the cabin, where a wonderful cold spring of the purest water I had ever tasted bubbled, we were starved, although we had eaten a snack along the way and were prepared with knapsacks of food for overnight. Even though the ranger wasn't home, the door to the cabin was unlocked, so we went in. A large pot of pinto beans and stew meat was cooking on the wood-burning stove. In the oven we found a big pan of biscuits browning.

The temptation was overwhelming. We just couldn't resist the delicious fragrance of the cooking food. There were eleven of us, and we were right in the midst of consuming the ranger's dinner when he suddenly walked in. It had been a couple of weeks since he had seen another human being, and he was happy to have even our company. He was a jolly man by the name of Woodward, who promptly put on another pot of beans, whipped up another batch of biscuits, and entertained us during the evening with tales about forest fires, mountain lions, and his life as a ranger. That night, some of us slept inside the cabin in our homemade sleeping bags, though some braver souls slept on the porch outside. Needless to say, at that elevation, even in late June it got pretty cold.

The next year, the Boy Scout camp was held at White House Canyon on the west side of the Santa Ritas. A small stream ran there also. For some reason we didn't have nearly as much fun as we had the year before at Gardner Canyon, but I did have one unforgettable experience. A brother scout, Andy Hollohan, and I killed twenty-seven rattlesnakes. We found a lair of them and cleaned them out. We skinned them, filled them with dry sand, hung them up to dry, and, with the heads still attached, brought the skins back to town and sold them to a Mrs. Holbert, who used them to make hatbands and belts. We got fifty cents apiece for them. (Incidentally, Andy Hollohan was the father of a recent member of the Arizona Supreme Court.)

The following year a permanent Boy Scout camp was established in the Catalina Mountains, near a large spring at the foot of Mt. Bigelow, which was connected to Soldiers Camp some four miles away by a trail, but no road. It was named Camp Lawton for James Lawton, a Tucson businessman who raised most of the money for it.

I was one of an advanced troop of Scouts chosen to start construction of the camp. The first thing we had to do was cut down several large pine trees, eighty or ninety feet tall. I remember that a boy by the name of Arthur Felix and I were given the job—and the honor—of cutting down the first tree. We sat on the ground on each end of a large cross-cut saw and sawed away until the tree toppled over, amid much shouting. I remained at the camp for a whole month, working on the crew that kept supplies flowing along the trail from Soldiers Camp aboard a stubborn burro. I often made two trips a day and knew the trail by heart.

I also worked with the professional cook, an affable black man from Tucson, preparing the meals for the sixty-eight scouts at the camp. When he took sick and had to leave the camp to return to Tucson, I was made the chief cook and bottle-washer—literally. With a bevy of helpers, I cooked for sixty-eight kids for five days. Don't ask me how I did it because I don't remember.

At the end of that camp, three of us guys, Don Hummell, who later became mayor of Tucson, Jim Davis, and I, decided to hike down the mountain. The trail ran through Sabino Canyon at the foot of the Catalinas, and the worst part of the trip was from the canyon over the July desert into town. Fortunately, my father drove out about halfway to Sabino and saved us the last seven miles of a thirty-three mile hike.

Occasional Floods despite Little Annual Rainfall

ANYONE WHO BELIEVES Tucson never has flood problems is sadly mistaken, even if the average annual rainfall is only ten to twelve inches.

The first flood I remember occurred in the winter of 1915. During December of that year, all of southern Arizona endured two or three weeks of heavy rainfall that caused the Santa Cruz River and other streams to run wild.

I remember seeing large sections of barns and other buildings floating down the Santa Cruz as well as large limbs of trees uprooted by the raging water. At that time there was only one bridge over the Santa Cruz. It was a red steel and wooden structure that crossed the river on West Congress Street.

The 1915 flood washed it out, isolating the Menlo Park area and, more important, cutting off St. Mary's Hospital from the rest of Tucson. There was no way to get supplies to the city's largest hospital. Community leaders recognized that something had to be done to get medicine, food, and other necessities to it.

I remember being on the east bank of the river near Congress with my dad when a special gun with a light string line was fired across the river to men who began pulling the lines of cord, and eventually heavy rope, to establish a kind of clothesline transportation system. Heavy wooden timbers were raised on each side of the river to lift the supplies above the level of the water. For two or three weeks, until the water flow subsided, that was how those on the west side of the river received their supplies and their mail.

A new bridge was constructed at the Congress Street location, and it wasn't long before a second bridge was built on St. Mary's Road.

The 1915 flood destroyed a popular recreational area known as Silver Lake, which had been created by the construction of an earthen dam across the Santa Cruz at about where Twenty-ninth Street now crosses the river. The river was diverted west of the lake and still was running as a small stream until the big flood in 1915, which completely washed out the lake.

I remember another series of heavy winter rains in December of 1922, which inundated all the southern half of the state. Although there was no serious loss from flooding, all the roads, which were dirt then, were muddy messes. I recall that after attending a Hi Y—the YMCA's club for high school boys—Conference in Phoenix, we drove back to Tucson over some of those very muddy roads, which were punctuated with many flooded dips. It took us seven hours to make the trip, which today takes less than two.

Most Tucsonans do not realize that under a large section of Tucson's business district run two sizable arroyos, over which they drive daily. These arroyos are open waterways through much of the eastern portion of Tucson, but in the areas west of Park Avenue, they have been covered for years. During heavy rains, they carry a great amount of rain water, which in the past would flood part of our business district.

One of the worst of those floods happened as a result of a very heavy summer storm in either 1940 or 1941. One of the largest arroyos was an open streambed that ran right next to the Tucson Electric Power Company plant on West Franklin Street, which was practically at its present site.

This huge storm dumped so much water into the area on the east side of town drained by this arroyo that it flooded the plant. The damage was so serious that Tucson was without electricity for six or seven days in August of that year.

The impact was catastrophic. No electricity meant no air-conditioning, no electric lights, and no electric traffic signals. Elevators in the few buildings that had them didn't work. People working in upper floors of the Valley Bank Building couldn't get to their offices, and guests in the Pioneer Hotel had to trudge many flights to their rooms. Many offices shut down. None of the theaters could operate without power, so we had no movies.

A basement full of new automobiles at O'Rielly Chevrolet, located next to the arroyo on North Sixth Avenue, was completely underwater. Other businesses suffered their own losses. It didn't take much politicking to convince the city council that something had to be done to avoid future flooding in the heart of the business district. The arroyos were soon covered, and nowadays the water runs through them with almost no one aware that it is happening.

But the most devastating flood ever to hit Tucson occurred in the summer of 1947. Eleven people died when the small Benson Highway bridge over the Julian Wash on the south side of town near the Veterans' Hospital washed away. The bridge was only about thirty feet long, so it seemed almost unbelievable that its loss could cause eleven people to die.

The heavy rain that caused the wash to overflow not only took out the bridge but also caused what is known as a flow of sheet water over the flat desert land in that area, which concealed the fact that the bridge was gone.

A local businessman by the name of Mela was the first to discover that the bridge was out. He was wise in driving so slowly that he was practically creeping along. When he reached the gap in the road, the front wheels of his car dropped over the bank but he was able to stop and get out of the car. He had been driving west and immediately went back down the road to make an effort to warn other drivers, but to no avail. They continued at full speed, not realizing that certain disaster awaited them.

Mela related the story of his frustrated efforts to warn drivers and said that he even got down on his knees in the shallow water, pleading with them to stop. Several cars went charging ahead, carrying those eleven people to their deaths before officials arrived on the scene and stopped traffic.

Tucson has experienced other floods that serve to remind residents that there can be too much water at times, even in an area that gets a relatively small amount of rainfall year after year. In 1983, and again in the early '90s, Tucson suffered severe floods that caused a considerable amount of damage. Each of these floods caused property owners living along the Rillito or the Pantano washes to demand that more bank areas be reinforced, all to the consternation of environmentalists.

Dooley's—Tucson's Most Popular Gathering Place

ABOUT THE TIME that I entered high school in 1920, Julius "Dooley" Bookman ran a small pool hall and cigar store on the west side of North Stone Avenue, halfway between Congress and Pennington Streets.

Dooley was a small, curly-haired fellow who always wore a big smile and who always made everybody who came into his place feel important. He was very popular, particularly among the younger men in town. Whenever they had a chance, they would gather at Dooley's to shoot the bull, exchange lies about their romantic conquests, talk about football, and play pool.

At noon time, many business and professional men would go to Dooley's to play pool or billiards and have a bite of lunch, which Dooley served over a small lunch counter. Dooley's was more like a club than a pool hall, and although ladies weren't ever seen there during the daytime, it was not uncommon for some of the wives or girl-

The redoubtable and natty
Dooley Bookman, owner of
Dooley's Pool Hall.

friends to accompany their husbands to Dooley's after hours, which
generally meant from ten at night till one in the morning.

My father had told my brother Frank and me that he didn't think
we should hang around there very much because there were always
some unsavory characters who frequented pool halls.

However, we protested and said that Dooley was a particular friend
of ours. We knew that he had come to Tucson to play drums in an orchestra for my father at the old Opera House. So he knew my father
quite well, of course, and my dad knew that he would keep an eye on
us, although he still didn't want us to spend too much time around
any pool hall at that time of our lives.

Dooley's was a hangout for the college kids who were a good deal
older than we were. They would gather there on Friday and Saturday
nights before their dates, go to a nearby shoeshine parlor, have their
shoes shined, and find out where they could, perhaps, find a bootleg-
ging joint that would sell them a flask of whiskey or some kind of
"hooch" to take with them on their dates.

The YMCA had a couple of pool tables, at which all of us kids
learned to play pool. When we could get to Dooley's and not worry

about our fathers finding us there, we would play pool. My cousin Dick Drachman was an excellent pool player and could beat any of us kids with ease.

In the fall of 1921, when I was fifteen and Dick was fourteen, he and I and a bunch of the kids were out carousing around the east side of town on Halloween Eve looking for some kind of trouble to get into. Nothing serious, but soon some of the kids began to throw rocks at the streetlights. When they broke one or two of them, Dick and I agreed that we didn't want any part of that gang so we left and went on downtown.

Dooley had just remodeled his storage basement and put three new pool tables in it. To celebrate its opening, he was having a tournament that night, the winner of which would be declared the pool champion of Tucson. Dick and I stopped by, knowing that there was going to be a lot of activity, and Dooley and some of his friends persuaded Dick to enter the tournament. I remember that Dick was wearing a mackinaw and when the pool tournament started, he handed it to me. My job would be to hold it for him all during the tournament.

Dick was by far the youngest entry in the tournament and also was, by far, the most sober. All the rest of the guys had been drinking and most of them had a snoot full of Tequila or something equally potent.

One after another, Dick beat them all. Several of them were actually better pool players, but because they were under the influence Dick beat them handily. When we left Dooley's to walk home, we were elated: Dick had won the pool championship of the entire city of Tucson.

But we didn't know what was in store for us.

The next morning, the *Arizona Daily Star* greeted us with a headline proclaiming that Dick Drachman was the new city pool champion. That's just what we didn't need!

Herb Drachman, Dick's father, was very hard on Dick most of the time and raised Holy Hell with him for violating his instructions to stay out of Dooley's. The fact that Dick had won the pool championship indicated to his old man that Dick not only had been at Dooley's on that occasion but probably many times, playing pool and learning to play very well.

The article that accompanied the headline noted that his cousin Roy was with him and was "holding his coat" while he competed in the tournament which, of course, sent a damning message to my dad that I had been there, too.

My father was a more reasonable and nicer sort of guy than Dick's dad and, though he gave me moderate hell, he rather laughed about the incident and knew that, deep down, Herb Drachman would be proud of his son but would well conceal it and be tough on him. Naturally, that was exactly what happened.

As I GREW older, I spent a lot of "legal" time at Dooley's. The Fox Theater, which I managed, backed up to his rear door and the pool hall became like a second office for me. I was never much of a pool player but I did enjoy playing it, as I did three-cushion billiards.

During the mid-1930s, the university hired a band director by the name of Joe DeLuca, who had traveled for many years as one of the top musicians with the world-famous Sousa Band, founded by John Philip Sousa himself. So having DeLuca become the band master at the university and a professor of music was quite a coup, and the community was excited to have him living here. Because he led the marching band both before the football game and during the half, he became a very well-known figure. He and his wife were a lovely couple, and his slight Italian accent gave him a bit of an exotic, European flavor.

He loved to play pool and would bring his wife down to Dooley's late at night when a few of us were gathered there to play and visit and have a bite to eat.

In the spring of 1935, a well-known Hollywood agent, Frank Orsatti, came to Tucson to cure himself of an asthma condition. Orsatti was one of the country's top film agents. Included in his stable of actors were Clark Gable, Edward G. Robinson, and many other stars under contract to MGM, the major studio in Hollywood at the time.

The manager of the MGM Studio was a man named Eddie Mannix, a good friend of mine. He called and told me that Frank Orsatti was coming to Tucson and asked if I would please look after him. Happily, this turned out to be more fun than responsibility.

Orsatti stayed at the Arizona Inn. As I got acquainted with him, I discovered that he loved to play pool. So during the daytime and for a couple of hours in the evening, we would pass the time at Dooley's. All of Dooley's regular fans became acquainted with him and enjoyed his company.

During those evenings at Dooley's, Joe DeLuca had gotten to know Orsatti and told him he thought Edward G. Robinson was the finest motion picture actor in the world. Orsatti didn't argue about that, of course. DeLuca also said that he hoped someday to meet Mr. Robinson.

Later that evening, Orsatti told me that he was going to try to get Robinson to come to Tucson and have dinner with Joe. He was as good as his word. Not long afterward, I found myself at the train station with Frank, meeting Edward G. Robinson.

Frank and I spent the day driving him around Tucson, avoiding any publicity about his visit. That evening, we went to Dooley's where Joe DeLuca was busy playing pool. We walked in and stood by the side of the pool table, not saying anything to Joe beyond a quick hello.

After we were there for a few minutes and Joe had made a pretty good shot, Robinson spoke up. "Nice shot, Joe!" he said. Joe whirled around, recognizing that somebody who sounded just like Edward G. Robinson had spoken to him.

When he saw who it was, he dropped his pool cue, threw his arms around Orsatti, thanked him for bringing Mr. Robinson down, and, of course, grabbed Mr. Robinson by both arms and practically assaulted him in his efforts to show his proper respect to such a great man.

Until Joe's sudden death in 1935, he never got over the fact that Mr. Robinson came to Tucson just to see him.

Business and Politics

Tucson Early Investments

As IN ALMOST every town in America, shysters have taken advantage, or tried to take advantage, of ambitious or adventurous Tucsonans seeking ways to make a bundle in a hurry. Over the seventy years that I've been involved in Tucson business affairs, I've seen some interesting, exciting, and dumb investments (or gambles) made by my fellow Tucsonans. I've even been involved in a couple myself.

One of the earliest I recall occurred around 1926, right after I had quit college and started managing the Rialto Theater. I was told by my father that a boyhood friend of his and other old-timers' had returned to town and was offering investors an opportunity to get in on a fabulous oil well deal in Louisiana. As I remember, the man's name was Bateman and he had been in the oil business for many years. He had returned to the Old Pueblo to give some old friends an opportunity to get in on the ground floor of a "can't miss" deal.

I remember that the land involved was forty acres in a hot oil field where several wells had been drilled and proven to be oil producers. Investment packages were offered in segments of $500 each. A sizable number of local investors bought several of them because of their confidence in Bateman. At the time I didn't have any money to invest, but, without telling my father, who was one of the investors, I borrowed $500 from his partner, Ben Goldsmith, and bought a segment in the new company. I just didn't want to miss out on such a bonanza investment.

A few weeks passed, and exciting news from Bateman in Louisiana began to arrive in Tucson. The first well had struck oil, and others were being drilled forthwith. These wells were striking oil at much shallower levels than California or even Texas wells, so they didn't take so long nor cost so much to drill.

The good news continued for several months, and we Tucson investors were excited about the profits that should flow for years from such magnificent wells. In fact, every one of the first eight drilled hit oil. The ninth didn't, but none of us was too upset about that bit of bad luck.

About that time, probably eight or nine months after he first returned to Tucson, Bateman came back and told a meeting of some twenty or thirty investors that he had worked out a very favorable deal to trade our 40-acre parcel for a 160-acre one in the same area. The new wells he'd dig there would mean that the value of our investment would be quadrupled immediately. Because some of our investors had gone to Louisiana and seen for themselves our already-producing wells, Bateman had no difficulty in convincing us that he was offering us a very good deal indeed. We went along with him, and the swap was made.

Several months went by with no news, good or bad, coming out of Louisiana about our new, larger oil field. However, when news eventually did begin to emerge, it was bad. The wells drilled on our new field were all dry holes. Soon it became apparent that we had been had, cheated by a crook by the name of Bateman.

A year or so later, a man came to the office in the Opera House seeking my father, who was in California for the summer. The man revealed himself to be an agent with the Justice Department, and he informed me he was assigned to investigate Bateman and his activities in Tucson. He wanted to know what I could tell him about Bateman, which wasn't much based on my personal experiences with him. So he asked me if I would take him to see General Manning, one of our town's most respected and important businessmen, who had also invested with Bateman.

I called General Manning and drove the agent down to the General's large estate in Snob Hollow, just west of north Main Street. We sat around the swimming pool for a couple of hours, during which the agent made copious notes of the general's comments. He told us that there was large amount of evidence that proved Bateman was a con man and predicted he would be found guilty and serve several years in a federal pen.

His prediction proved to be correct. Bateman was indeed locked up several years. That didn't get any of our money back, but it was satisfying to know that the son of a gun was not running loose and cheating other friends or investors.

About five years after the experience with the bad oil deal, another opportunity came to light. This one involved an invention that someone had developed to align automobile wheels. A sample of the machine had already been produced and tested by the brother of Chet Vasey Sr., who ran two or three service stations in Tucson and was one of the promoters of the equipment known as the Alignometer. Theoretically, it was supposed to be able to heat the axles of the car and bend them, if needed, to produce perfect alignment of the wheels and tires.

Quite a few local investors put money into the deal, including my father, who had just sold his interest in two Tucson theaters. He gave me and my brother Frank several hundred shares in the new company holding the patents on the Alignometer as bonuses for our part in selling the theaters. Unfortunately, the invention didn't prove to be valuable, to say the least. There were no crooked actions on the parts of any of those promoting the equipment, but, nevertheless, the investments were worthless.

A number of years later, another group of Tucson professionals and businessmen was taken to the cleaners by perhaps the most fascinating con artist of all, a middle-aged woman who proved to be one hell of a saleslady, not just once but a second time as well.

She was not terribly attractive, but she had a great gift of gab that helped her penetrate the inner offices of attorneys and dentists. She had developed a story, complete with photographs, maps, and mining reports, about a secret cave in the mountains south of Tucson containing hundreds of millions of dollars in gold bars that had been hidden there by Indians from Mexico many years before.

She took hundreds of thousands of dollars from her professional friends and others who had great faith in her. She was using their money, she claimed, to remove avalanche rock and soil that had recently blocked the entrance to her Aladdin's cave. Later, there would be more rock and more dirt, which again blocked access to the riches. Her suckers would believe her and come up with more money.

One prominent dentist admitted to newspaper reporters that he invested over $200,000 with her. Several businessmen told similar stories of investing heavily with her and claimed that she was an honest mining prospector who had just had a lot of bad luck. Still in the game, she produced a photograph of a horse with the very worst swayback imaginable, claiming that the poor animal's condition was caused by the heavy loads of gold bars it had carried from Mexico to the cave. She continued to maintain that her old maps proved the location of the cave was truly authentic.

She was arrested, however, and her trial was given a great deal of space in the local press. Names of the prominent investors, several of whom appeared as witnesses, were splashed over the news columns. She was found guilty and sentenced to a relatively short term in the state penitentiary at Florence.

One of her unfortunate investors happened to work for me as an engineer at the Fox Theater, which I was managing. He had lost, what was for him, a lot of money in her scheme, but that didn't keep him from testifying for her at her trial. After she started serving time at Florence, he and his wife would drive up and take food and other things she wanted to her. Later, when her term ended and she came back to Tucson, they even allowed her to move in with them. I talked to them about her, and they swore she really knew where the gold bars were hidden and had done nothing wrong. A few other investors stuck by her, also, and helped support her, but she never produced anything for them but a lot of baloney.

Kansas City Investor Invades Tucson

In 1934, BARNEY Goodman, an important Kansas City businessman, bought in one fell swoop the Santa Rita Hotel, Tucson's second most important downtown hostelry; the Consolidated National Bank, the city's largest financial institution; and the Consolidated Bank Building, one of the city's two high-rise structures.

This shook the fabric of the business community. These assets had been owned for sometime by a mining man by the name of T. N. McCauley. McCauley had invested heavily in a copper mine, the Dos Cabezas, and had imported two or three executives from Boston to help him run the mine, the hotel, and the bank. Two of the men remained here for the rest of their lives and were important additions to the community: Walter Clapp and Stanley Williamson, who later became Realtors.

The third, who was brought in to run the bank and whose name I shall not use, was not very popular and was considered to be somewhat shady in his dealings. He didn't move here but would come into town quite often. The Consolidated Bank had installed a large bell on the exterior of the building as part of a new burglar alarm system. Several times when it went off accidentally and woke up the whole downtown area, the local wags would say that so-and-so (the bad guy banker) must be in town.

For some reason, state banking authorities did not approve Goodman as the operator of the Consolidated Bank. So he sold the bank and its high-rise building to the Valley National Bank, Arizona's largest, which had wanted to enter the Tucson market for some time. This was a good deal for the community as well as for Valley National Bank. However, before selling, Goodman removed a bundle of promissory notes owed by local people who had not been able to pay off their loans from the bank. He knew that many of the notes would eventually be paid off.

He began calling on these debtors and worked out long-term payoffs with many of Tucson's prominent businessmen who found that Barney Goodman was a tough businessman but one with whom they could work. It gave him a chance to quickly become acquainted with many local people.

Barney Goodman immediately became very active in the operation of the Santa Rita. He imported three experienced hotelmen from Kansas City and began spending money improving the property and refurbishing the lobby and many of the rooms. Such improvements were overdue.

He spent quite a bit of money remodeling the dining room and converting it into a nightclub. He imported a dance band, brought in entertainers, and gave Tucson a touch of class it badly needed.

He converted a mezzanine meeting room into the Santa Rita Club, a cocktail lounge with a series of musical entertainers.

The three executives he brought in were Ed Meyers, a financial man, Benny Klein, the food and liquor manager, and, by far the most flamboyant of the trio, Nick Hall, the general manager of the Santa Rita. Nick was a large man, about six foot three, who weighed about 250 pounds and possessed a booming voice.

This whole operation kind of shook the town up. Everyone wondered how the hotel could possibly afford not only the improvements but also the costs of bringing in high-powered management people. I remember that most people expected that the hotel would operate some kind of gambling racket.

It took a while, about a year, for the community to realize that these new guys were for real and were actually pretty nice sorts. Nick Hall hit town like a tornado. He had been manager for many years of the San Angelo Hotel in San Antonio and was acquainted with many of the cattlemen in that area as well as here. The Santa Rita had always been popular with the local cowboys and ranchers. Nick played up to them and made them feel at home.

In fact, he and some of the ranchers started the Mountain Oyster Club, which people from all walks of life joined, although it especially attracted the cattle people. It operated in the basement off the lobby of the hotel and soon became a popular drinking and dining spot.

Nick recognized the importance of courting the movie companies that were coming in and out of Tucson seeking production locations. He helped them find interesting locations on ranches and other spots all over southern Arizona. The Santa Rita Hotel became the unofficial headquarters for many film crews.

Nick really hit the jackpot when it was decided to make the movie of Clarence Buddington Kelland's best-seller, *Arizona*, here in Tucson. Kelland lived in Phoenix, and the story was based on the history of Tucson.

This was by far the most important production made in Tucson, because a whole town had to be built. The set became Old Tucson, which was built here by Columbia Pictures in the Tucson Mountains. A man by the name of Jim Pratt was in charge of the construction, which took several months and meant that production crews were here all that time. The shooting of the movie went on for a long time, too.

This activity poured a lot of money into Tucson during the Depression, when it was badly needed. All of this brought recognition to Nick Hall, the Santa Rita, and, of course, to Barney Goodman, though many of the stars of the companies making pictures here would prefer to stay at the Arizona Inn rather than be with the movie crews at the Santa Rita.

Goodman's entry into Tucson was important and helped improve our economy when the town was suffering badly, and the entertainment at the Santa Rita Hotel beneficially boosted the morale of the community.

Barney Goodman was a plenty smart hombre. He purchased the Chapman Park Hotel on Wilshire Boulevard in Los Angeles, right across the street from the famous Ambassador Hotel. It covered a full block and consisted of a series of buildings containing suites and rooms on a well-landscaped block right in the heart of the city. Barney told me that he paid only $50,000 down for the entire property. He bought it during the war, right after a Japanese submarine fired a shell that landed on a beach in northern California. Some people panicked, fearing the Japanese would soon invade the West Coast, and wanted to get out before that happened. Doubtless, one of those who panicked was the man who owned the Chapman Park and sold it to Goodman for a very low price. Barney had a long-term contract to pay off the balance of the purchase price, but the $50,000 was all the money he ever put in the deal. The hotel, which was worth millions, earned enough to provide him with the money to pay it off.

Barney later bought the famous old landmark near San Diego, the Hotel Del Coronado. He owned and operated it for many years. It was a popular summer retreat for not only Tucsonans but people from all over the world.

Barney Goodman made his mark upon Tucson, Los Angeles, and San Diego. His son, Jack Goodman, still resides here and, although he maintains a low profile, has played an important role in watching over the still-popular Mountain Oyster Club on North Stone Avenue. He has an outstanding collection of works by famous western artists.

Early Publicity Stunts

IN THE 1940s, while I was running the Tucson Sunshine Climate Club, the community's tourist promotion organization, we were constantly trying to figure out ways to get publicity for Tucson.

We had two full-time photographers working for us, taking pictures of prominent visitors to be sent to their hometown papers to get Tucson's name mentioned. They also took pictures of local newsmaking events such as beauty contests, golf tournaments, rodeos, Mexican festivals, and such. Sometimes, we had to stage special events to create "picture stories" to make the press.

One such event was an idea that a professional camera reporter and I figured would create quite a story for the press across the nation, and even overseas. The reporter's name was Charles Herbert. He had moved here and built a home in the foothills after traveling the world for *Pathe News* and the *March of Time*. He knew how to tell a story with a camera.

A large conference of southwestern Indian tribes was being held in Tucson with several thousand Native Americans gathering for the four- or five-day conference. Because this was during World War II, we came up with the idea of having all of the tribes adopt a measure condemning the swastika as a symbol on any of their art objects such as baskets, Indian rugs, blankets, etc., because of the use of it by the Nazis.

First, we had to reach the proper chieftains and get them to get their elders to agree to the idea. This took some doing because some tribes weren't a bit interested in becoming involved in such a controversial matter. However, we got two or three tribes to agree to ban the swastika and that was all we needed.

We gathered some discarded draperies, a couple of old throw rugs, some hatboxes from the White House Department Store (which we painted with swastikas to make them look like Indian baskets), and some material with which to build a fire.

We borrowed some Indian headdresses with long tails of feathers from an Indian curio store. About nine o'clock one night, we drove out to the San Xavier Mission and prepared to set a bonfire. I knew that Native American youngsters of high school age played basketball on an outdoor court in back of the mission every night. We recruited them for small stipends to become players in our story, which would show tribal members in their headdresses burning their art objects to destroy the now-banned swastika.

We built a large bonfire and had the Indians dance around it throwing "baskets," blankets, and rugs with swastikas onto the fire. All this made a colorful set of pictures in front of the lovely mission, which formed a perfect background.

We wrote appropriate captions for the photographs and news articles, then sent them off to the Associated Press in New York and to eight or ten major newspapers. They made the front page in nearly every newspaper in the country. In fact, we got phone calls asking for more pictures. We had to replay the whole act again the next night and, of course, added a couple of new twists. We got a world of publicity for Tucson.

ANOTHER PUBLICITY STUNT Charlie Herbert and I cooked up got Tucson major publicity in an important national publication.

We designed a girl's bathing suit made of cactus for a pretty young model to wear. That probably sounds like an impossible task, but we worked it out.

We cut four or five flat prickly pear cactus pads and removed all of the thorns from one side so that when the pads laid against the young lady's thighs, they'd be smooth. That provided the material for the skirt portion of the bathing suit, which we hung from a heavy ribbon around the model's waist.

For the halter, we cut the top off two small saguaro cactuses, hollowed them out by removing the pulp, then attached them to a ribbon which fit around the model's neck.

We found a nice poolside setting for the cactus-clad young lady and took a series of camera shots that not only showed the model full-figure but showed how we made the cactus bathing suit. We bundled the photos with appropriate captions and sent them to *Life* magazine.

Two weeks later, *Life* ran a full page of pictures and a story about Tucson's cactus bathing suit. At that time, a full-page ad in *Life* magazine was priced at a whopping $10,000. A few local stuffy folks weren't crazy about that type of publicity for the Old Pueblo, but it was generally well accepted.

A couple of weeks later, a letter to the editor of *Life* noted that everyone was aware "that men never make passes at girls who wear glasses" but that now we should add "that men never practice on girls who wear cactus."

In 1944, travel was considered a luxury if it wasn't for business or the war effort. Gasoline and tires were rationed, and both were difficult to get. Hotel rooms were nearly impossible to reserve. Travel for pleasure was frowned upon, even if you were able to get gasoline.

Because the cattle business and farming were essential industries in the war effort, cattlemen and farmers were able to obtain supplies for their business. However, attending a convention was another story. With no hotel rooms available in the winter of 1944, the annual Cattlemen's Convention, scheduled to be held in Tucson, was canceled.

But the Rodeo Parade Committee, composed of about twenty-five of us who had worked together for over twenty years, thought that there was a way the Cattlemen's Convention could be held here if certain things could be done.

Since there'd be no hotel rooms available, the visitors would have to bring their bedrolls or their campers, which could be set up in the barns at the rodeo field where we stored our parade vehicles. For meals we would sponsor barbecues if the visitors would supply most of the meat. We would do the cooking and serve the food.

Having been a cook at a large Boy Scout camp many years before, I knew how to cook breakfast for large numbers of people. There were going to be between 250 and 300 people attending the convention, so when I agreed to fix breakfasts for two mornings I realized I was committing to quite a chore.

I had to borrow utensils and other equipment from Davis-Monthan Air Force Base because I needed huge pots and pans in which I could make pancakes, scramble eggs, cook ham and bacon, bake biscuits, serve coffee, and so on. Naturally, I had several volunteers, but I had to get up in the middle of the night to go out to Shamrock Dairy to pick up fifty gallons of milk and cream for coffee. Most of the stuff was donated.

I made over a thousand pancakes, cooked I-don't-know-how-many eggs, made several hundred biscuits, and supervised a crew of about fifteen helpers. So far as I know, no one got sick or died from my cooking.

The evening barbecues went off as planned and the cattlemen were happy with their convention.

There was, however, one foul-up on my part. After the second barbecue, there was a very large pot of Mexican frijoles left over, which, I was then, and still am, crazy about. I got a large gallon jar, filled it with beans, and put it in the trunk of my Pontiac.

Then I completely forgot about it.

Three days later when I went out to get in my car late in the afternoon, I noticed the worst smell I had ever encountered in my life. The gallon bottle of beans had exploded and sprayed every inch of the trunk. I immediately took the car to get it washed and cleaned, but it was a lost cause.

I bought a bottle of cheap perfume and sprayed the trunk thoroughly, so it didn't stink quite so bad when I took it to the used car lot to sell it. I absolutely had to get rid of that car—no one could stand the smell. Luckily, I'd already been drafted, and I left for the army ten days later.

How Planning, Zoning, and a Freeway Came to Tucson

ONE MATTER IN Tucson that is and has been on a front burner for most of the last fifty years is the subject of land use and land planning, as it has for nearly every growing city in the western and southern states.

Up until the mid-thirties, there were no laws governing land planning in Arizona. In fact, zoning of land was not legal in the United States until 1926, when the U.S. Supreme Court validated a zoning ordinance enacted by the state of Ohio and the city of Cleveland. Land use planning had been permitted, but, without the legal teeth provided by zoning, it was generally not followed when owners began to use their land.

In order for a city to have the authority to enact land use and zoning laws, the state had to permit it to do so through enabling legislation or referendum. In Arizona there were no such laws until the 1930s. Knowledgeable people in both Tucson and Phoenix were cognizant of the new laws permitting zoning and began a joint campaign to have the Arizona legislature adopt appropriate enabling acts for the two largest cities in the state.

It was not easy to get the legislature to act. Many people, particularly the owners of large land parcels and the real estate developers, fought the legislation and certainly delayed it. However, the legislature did approve it.

But that was only half the battle. Getting the city councils in each community to move forward with local ordinances was another fight. Money had to be budgeted, planners employed, legal measures drafted by local city attorneys, and, to meet a complicated set of regulations contained in the enabling legislation, a considerable amount of research regarding existing land uses had to be completed.

In the meantime, those of us in Tucson who had been urging the legislature to move forward with the enabling legislation formed the Tucson Regional Plan, Inc. to provide an organized support program to urge the Tucson City Council to move forward on planning and zoning. It was a futile effort for several years, with strong opposition from various people, most of whom were not well informed about the need for and the benefits of land planning.

The Tucson Regional Plan launched a campaign to raise what was then a lot of money, $60,000, to pay for a Master Land Use Plan to be developed by a planning firm with a national reputation. The Ladislaw Segoe firm of Cincinnati was contracted with to produce it. Mr. Segoe brought to Tucson a small staff, headed by Andrew Faure, to make the necessary studies, do the research, and prepare the plan for all the land lying within the city limits. The team spent eighteen months producing the necessary data, land maps, and zoning laws.

Naturally there was a great deal of interest in the whole exercise and especially the impact it would have on properties owned by local people. It took some "politicking" by the proponents to get the city council to move forward and adopt Segoe's plan and the necessary zoning for it. All during this time, I was not in the real estate business, but, as a citizen, I did participate in a minor way to do what I could to move the process along. There were many people, such as Dr. Donald Hill, John Murphey, Dr. Paul Holbrook, George Chambers, Monte Mansfeld, Hubert D'Autremont, William Dunipace, Margaret Knight, Kitty Morehead, and several others, who really were responsible for pushing the legislation and raising the money to pay for the master plan.

Andy Faure, who came to Tucson with the Segoe organization, remained here, first for a year or two to properly present the plan to the community, and later moved here to become planning director for the city of Tucson. The plan was given to the community by Tucson Regional Plan, Inc. without charge and served for many years as the guiding map for the use and development of property within the Tucson city limits.

As development proceeded both inside and outside the city limits, it became abundantly clear that planning and zoning were having an impact on the quality of the kind of development we were seeing. That was particularly noticeable along some of the major streets, such as East Speedway and South Sixth Avenue, where various kinds of unattractive buildings and developments with gaudy signs easily identified the boundary between planned and unplanned areas.

It wasn't long before many people became aware of the need for planning and zoning to be applied to areas in the county, too, if the community were to continue to grow in a fashion that would create a good lifestyle for its citizens. People in Phoenix were likewise recognizing the need for county zoning, and soon the groups favoring land planning and zoning in the two communities organized their forces to convince the legislature of the need to plan and zone land areas located outside the jurisdiction of cities.

Again, many of us began traveling to the capital to lobby the legislature on behalf of planning and zoning authorities for the two largest counties in Arizona, Maricopa and Pima. Counties with smaller populations disliked the idea of planning and zoning, and only by compromising with them did the legislation pass.

The next problem was getting the Pima County Board of Supervisors to adopt proper planning and zoning ordinances. Ranchers and farmers in both of the two affected counties strenuously fought land use regulation. Again, considerable compromise was needed to get the ordinances adopted. Homer Boyd, chairman of the Pima County Board of Supervisors, was chiefly responsible for their adoption, despite strong opposition from real estate interests and owners of large land areas.

After the ordinances were adopted, the local association of Realtors circulated petitions calling for a referendum to overturn the action by the supervisors. An election was scheduled, and those favoring planning and zoning had to raise substantial funds to battle those opposed to the measures. I was appointed chairman of those favoring the position taken by the supervisors, but I was the only Realtor (I had become one in 1947) on that side of the issue. All of the others were organized in opposition to planning and zoning. I wasn't very popular at gatherings of real estate brokers but I was convinced the entire community should be planned if we were to create the proper kind of an environment for the future here.

Fortunately, the electorate defeated the attempt to overthrow county zoning, and it became effective immediately. Soon the city and county planning and zoning departments were consolidated, and Andy Faure became director of planning for both the city and the county. However, it wasn't long before it became apparent that the combination wasn't working as effectively as it was hoped, and the department was again split.

A few years later, Tucson's downtown streets became a nightmare to negotiate. Stone Avenue was part of the main route through town. The chief roads leading in and out of Tucson were directly connected to Stone, so all traffic traveling the federal highway system drove right down it. It was the busiest north-south street in the city for local traffic alone, even without all the trucks and trailers, the campers, and all the other cross-country vehicles.

Finally, in the 1950s, at the urging of President Eisenhower, Congress adopted a historic bill creating a program for a nationwide highway system connecting practically every city in America to freeways or parkways as a gigantic defense measure.

Money was being made available in every state to kick off the program. Arizona was allotted $900,000, which seemed to be a small amount even then, but it at least would enable the state to become part of the new system of freeways. Naturally, Phoenix had first shot at getting the money but, for some strange reason, didn't want to construct a roadway that would permit interstate traffic to bypass the city.

Some of us in Tucson thought it would make a lot of sense to construct a freeway somewhere so that the traffic could be diverted from the heart of the business district. Big trucks and trailers, especially some carrying heavy loads of all kinds of hazardous materials, including dynamite from the powder plant at Benson, should be able to bypass downtown Tucson, we believed. We decided to go after the money for the first part of the new freeway system in Arizona.

The Arizona highway engineer had the authority to decide how and where the money would be spent. Jack Proctor, who was then operator of the Pioneer Hotel and also a member of the Arizona Highway Commission; Fred Stofft, president of the Tucson Chamber of Commerce; Mayor Happy Houston; and I drove up to Phoenix one day to meet with the highway engineer, Curley Lefebre, who happened to be from Tucson. He told us that the $900,000 allotted to Arizona had been refused by Phoenix, so if we wanted it to construct a freeway around Tucson it was available. He pointed out, however, that the money could be used for planning and construction of the new roadway but the money to acquire the right-of-way had to come from the city of Tucson.

Although we had the mayor there to agree to that proposal, we recognized that the money for the right-of-way had to be provided through a bond issue, requiring a vote by the electorate. Nonetheless, we came back to Tucson feeling that we had accomplished an important step to relieve the bad traffic condition in our downtown area. We soon found out, though, that it was not a unanimous belief in the community that it would be wise to remove the interstate traffic from Stone.

The city council called for an election to approve the bond issue to raise the funds needed to acquire the right of way. Opposition immediately came forth, contending that the diversion of interstate traffic off of principal streets was a serious mistake. As I remember, the bond amount was less than a million dollars but many downtown property owners and businesspeople were opposed to the idea of a bypass freeway under any circumstances.

For some reason, I was made chairman of the committee promoting the bond issue. I appeared before all the civic clubs, speaking for the bonds, and also engaged in a debate on the radio with Glenn Harrison, a downtown property owner. Anyway, to complete the story, the bond issue was approved by a healthy majority despite the opposition from some of our leading downtown businesspeople.

It wasn't long before other federal funds were available from the huge program, which was now affecting every city in the nation. Phoenix soon realized their mistake and began to take their share of federal funds as they became available.

Pima County's Lawbreaking Attorney and Sheriff

WE HAVE BEEN fortunate over the years here in Tucson to have had few problems with crooked public officials or with criminal elements that have attempted to bribe local officials, but there was a time back a good many years ago when both our county attorney and the county sheriff were involved in a blatant attempt to set up a business they controlled and expected to make money for them.

Bryce Wilson was the properly elected county attorney and Jerry Martin, a native born Tucsonan, was the sheriff about fifty years ago. They were elected in 1946. They were both popular men and were easily elected. Bryce was a member of the El Rio Country Club, a graduate of the University of Arizona, and a handsome young man. He was married to a nice young lady and had a baby boy. Jerry's family were long-time Tucsonans and well respected.

But something went wrong. Of course, the positions they held were important, and they were the principal law enforcement officers of the county. If either one of them had resisted the temptation to pick up some tainted money the problem would have been avoided, but they both apparently agreed to the unlawful acts.

Inadvertently, I was involved in the action that put a stop to their unlawful business, which was known as the "W & M Ranch," located in the northwestern residential area west of Oracle Road.

Rumors were rampant in the Tucson downtown business circles that some funny business was going on at the courthouse, where both the county attorney and sheriff's offices were located. Wilson always liked to have his daily alcoholic drinks, and Martin was of similar tastes. They both were reported to be drinking heavily and doing some uncharacteristic things. Bryce Wilson was always inclined to be a "lady's man," and rumors had him involved with a professional "lady of the night" by the name of Dolores Raines. She was a dark-haired beauty.

The pair of public officials got carried away with their power and became far too brazen with their unlawful business of owning and operating a "house of ill repute," known as the "W & M Ranch" (for Wilson and Martin). Dolores Raines was the madam and manager of the operation. As has been said for all the time I've been in this world, and I'm sure for all ages, whenever such operations or gambling or illegal hard liquor sales are allowed over a period of time, you can be sure someone is being paid off, meaning some law officials are being bribed by the operators to permit the unsavory businesses.

There was an identifying sign in front of the "W & M Ranch," which operated in the midst of a nice residential area across the street from the home of Mr. and Mrs. Clifford Goldsmith, who was a writer and a playwright of a Broadway play at the time. Goldsmith is best known for his long-running radio family show, *Henry Aldrich,* with its renowned "coming Mother" line. Cliff and his wife, Kay, lived in Tucson for many years and were well liked.

One evening at a party at Mildred "Mickey" Loew's home, I was asked by Cliff Goldsmith if, during the many times he was required to be in New York while his play was in rehearsal for its Broadway opening, I would be willing to serve as a contact for his wife, Kay, if she felt she needed help with some kind of a problem. I assured him I would be happy to do so. Little did I expect to hear from her so soon.

A couple of weeks later, she called me one morning and said that around daybreak a couple of soldiers had driven up to her house and asked her nine-year-old son "Is this the whore house?" and when the boy said he didn't know what they were talking about, they proceeded to tell him about the facts of life of what they were looking for. Kay was incensed and said that it had been going on for far too long and that she wanted something done about it.

I told her I would make a couple of phone calls and see what could be done about it. I called Bill Johnson, copublisher of the *Tucson Citizen*, and asked if I could see him. He invited me to come to his office. We were very good friends, and I knew pretty well what his reactions would be.

I told him the story of that morning's event at the "W & M Ranch." He said he had been hearing rumors from his staff of reporters about what had been going on at the offices of the county attorney and sheriff. When I finished my tale, he said, "That does it. We must do something."

And he did. That afternoon's edition of the *Citizen* had a front-page, boldface headline and an appropriate article written by one of the *Citizen* reporters. An editorial appeared in that same issue of the *Citizen*, demanding an investigation of both the county attorney and the sheriff and their blatant unlawful operations.

To make a long story short, an investigation took place. This was in the fall of 1950. Both Wilson and Martin were up for reelection and had the temerity to run for office despite the furor regarding the ongoing investigation. They were both defeated at the polls. In April of 1951 they were charged with breaking several laws. Wilson left town and moved with his small family "down south" somewhere and disappeared into the woodwork. Martin remained here but never ran for office again. I don't know what eventually happened to him.

Over the years Tucson has seen short periods when houses of prostitution have operated here but never nearly so openly as when the "W & M Ranch" operated on the northwest side of town under the protection of Bryce and Jerry.

Hughes Comes to Tucson

THE ANNOUNCEMENT IN January of 1951 that the Hughes Company (now Raytheon) was coming to Tucson with its large electronics plant was the culmination of efforts that had been ongoing for over a year and a half.

To start at the beginning of the story, however, we have to go back to 1947 when Axel Johnson and his friend walked into my real estate office on West Pennington Street and told me they wanted to rent office space where he and his friend Nate Kendall could set up a construction company to build apartments and other buildings here. Axel

Perusing the contract they secretly negotiated to bring Hughes Aircraft (now Raytheon) to Tucson in 1951 are, *left to right* standing, Homer Boyd, Ed Goyette, and Monte Mansfield; *seated,* Roy and Mayor Joe Nieman. *Reginald Russell photo.*

was an architect, and Nate was a building contractor. They had been operating in the Denver area but had decided to move to Tucson and start their company. We were able to find an office for them, and they began looking for property on which to build some apartments.

Axel Johnson was a particularly nice guy and when his wife joined him a few weeks later, our families soon became good friends. We learned that they liked trout fishing and, with our two children, we made several trips to the White Mountains in the northeastern part of Arizona with them.

Axel and Nate were busily working on plans and specs for a 100-unit apartment building they hoped to build near Country Club Road. Unfortunately, financing such buildings in Tucson was difficult at that time. After about a year, they had to fold up their plans and move back to Denver, but they had fallen in love with Tucson and really hated to leave, promising they'd return someday.

Axel and his wife, Jimmie, returned the following year and attempted to set up a business in construction, but again, after several months, pulled up stakes and took off for other parts. He again said he'd return someday and make Tucson his home. He told me that he would get a large company to establish a plant here and become its manager—and that's just what he did. But I'm getting ahead of my story. . . .

Axel had been employed by the Ford Motor Co. in Detroit and was one of the "Whiz Kids," who were headed by future defense secretary Robert McNamara and Tex Thornton. They were doing some unusual things with Ford in the electronics field. After his unsuccessful ventures in Tucson, he returned to Detroit and Ford.

One day he called me and said that he was on his way to Los Angeles, where he had been offered a job. He was going to have a two-hour layover at the Tucson airport and wanted to talk to me. The job had been offered to him by Tex Thornton, who was now with the Howard Hughes Company in Los Angeles. Axel said he wanted to find out what I thought about his accepting it and moving to L.A. I met him and told him it sounded like a great offer, because he would be in charge of all construction for Hughes, which he said was on the threshold of a major expansion program. I urged him to accept the offer, which he did.

Now the plot thickens. Axel advised me that as part of Hughes's expansion program, he was designing buildings that their electronics division would be occupying. But most important were his instructions to begin the design of a large electronics plant of over a half million square feet, which Hughes would build at a city several hundred miles off the Pacific Coast. Axel made a trip to Tucson to plan strategy to get his company to select Tucson, his favorite city, as the place for the plant to be located. He told me that the decision about where the plant would be built would be one that would involve many Hughes department heads.

In order for them to know something about Tucson, he wanted me to have the Chamber of Commerce mail brochures and favorable materials regarding the Old Pueblo directly to them without mentioning the reason they were sent. He said that over the next several months he would ascertain who was likely to be important in the decision-making process, and, as he got the information, he would forward it to me to be relayed to the Chamber of Commerce. He was serving as a "fifth columnist," working on the inside for Tucson. This continued for almost a year, and the chamber sent a great deal of material about Tucson to Culver City.

At that time I was very much involved with the Del Webb Company, which was headquartered in Phoenix but which had a large office in Los Angeles where Del lived. I was in Phoenix every week visiting the Webb company executives about real estate, for which I was a consultant to them. The top executives were aggressively pursuing contracts for construction almost anyplace in the country.

I told L. C. "Jake" Jacobson, president of the Webb company, about the plans Hughes had for considerable construction work in the immediate future. He was fascinated with the prospect of establishing a relationship with Hughes and becoming their principle contractor. He had met Axel Johnson once when Jake came to Tucson in connection with their Pueblo Gardens project. He had his L.A. office check on the Hughes Company and learned that Axel Johnson did, indeed, have charge of construction for it. He called me and wanted to know how well I knew Axel, and when I told him that we were close friends, he asked me if I would help the Webb Company get its foot in the door with him.

Of course I assured him I would. For the next three weekends, Jake had his company plane pick me up in Tucson on Friday afternoon and join him in L.A. to entertain Axel and Jimmie, which hopefully would lead to construction contracts for Webb. As a result of these efforts, Del Webb became acquainted with Howard Hughes, and over the next twenty years the Webb Company did over a billion dollars' worth of work for Hughes, generally on a "cost-plus" basis.

On January 12, 1951, I received a call from Del asking me to meet a couple of men from the Hughes Company, who would be arriving at the Phoenix airport in about three hours to make a survey of Phoenix, Tucson, Albuquerque, and El Paso as possible sites for a very large electronics plant to be built by Hughes in a southwestern town not too far from their plant in Culver City. Del said he had just left the Hughes offices and had stopped at the first phone booth he came across, and the matter was a very hush-hush deal. He told me that his company's two planes were available for use in visiting the various cities. He said I'd better pack a bag of clothes, as I'd be busy for a few days.

I called my wife and had her pack me a bag of clothes and hurry down to my office. As soon as I received it, I took off for Phoenix. I met the plane carrying the Hughes men, and thus began the story of how Hughes eventually selected the site for the new plant at Tucson. For the next ten days I was busy traveling between Tucson and Phoenix.

The executives from the Hughes Company conducted themselves differently from any other men I had ever dealt with. They were very suspicious that there were loads of people who wanted to know what the Hughes Company was up to. This attitude no doubt came down from the very top of the company, which, of course, was Howard Hughes himself. He was a strange character in many ways and no doubt influenced the thinking and conduct of his executives. As an example, when we came to Tucson to talk to people connected with the airport where the company was looking at land, or the city or county people key to Hughes's decision making, the Hughes men insisted on not meeting in anyone's office. Instead, we met several times in hangars at the airport, or at the home of Monte Mansfeld, who was the chairman of the Tucson Airport Authority. And we'd meet only at night so that no one could see who was coming and going.

One night when their chief negotiator, a top commander in the U.S. Army Air Corps during the previous war, General Ira Eaker, arrived in town in a Hughes Company plane, we went to the Pioneer Hotel, where we had reserved a suite for him. While we were looking at maps and discussing the airport land and other details, he suddenly hushed us all and asked if the room "was secure." It looked as if it was to me, but a couple of the Hughes people started looking for microphones in back of the drapes and pictures, up in the light fixtures, under the bed, and behind the furniture. He said that we should pick up our papers and maps and go to a restaurant where we could sit in a back booth and finish our conversation, just to be safe. We did exactly that, in hushed tones.

That was their modus operandi all during the time they were investigating both Tucson and Phoenix. In Tucson we established relations between the Hughes people with Mayor Joe Nieman and Chairman Homer Boyd of the Pima County Board of Supervisors, and of course with Monte Mansfeld, at whose home we met on several evenings.

During this time the Hughes Company sent several small teams of people to check on many things in both Tucson and Phoenix. (By this time they seemed not to be interested in Albuquerque or El Paso.) They investigated housing conditions and costs, the prices of fruits and vegetables in the markets, the quality of schools, cultural opportunities, entertainment possibilities, and everything else that would affect their employees. They were curious about the labor force among better-educated people, and particularly people who knew something about electronics, radios, and even watchmaking. They were interested in learning about the engineering and electronics departments at the University of Arizona. Of particular concern was the price of vacant or raw land. We soon found out why.

In Phoenix we usually met with the top executive of the Chamber of Commerce and one or two leading citizens. But once, Hughes people were invited to a meeting with a group of about a dozen business leaders. I was casually acquainted with most of them and knew they were very unhappy when I sat in on their meeting with the Hughes executives, but I was determined that they would have to stick to the facts if they compared the two cities. They made their pitch in a very professional way and it was quite impressive. I had difficulty in estimating the impact they had on their visitors, and we never discussed the matter after that meeting.

As I said before, this investigation went on for ten days. Finally, one night at about ten-thirty, I drove General Eaker to Monte Mansfeld's house, where we had scheduled a meeting with Mayor Joe Nieman, supervisors' chairman Homer Boyd, and Ed Goyette, secretary of the Tucson Chamber of Commerce. We were sitting on the floor of Monte's living room looking at maps of the airport and surrounding property. The Tucson Airport Authority, through Monte, had told the Hughes people they could acquire, on a long-term ground lease, a parcel of approximately 500 acres, on which Hughes planned to build its plant.

After General Eaker's questions were answered to his satisfaction, he said, " 'The boss' has decided that Tucson is where the new plant will be built. However, there's one thing that he wants. He's tired of having people spying on and photographing our operations from nearby areas. We must have options on a mile-wide strip of property along the east border of the airport, and a mile-wide strip along the north side. We're not concerned about the area to the south because it's federal land, and to the west is the Indian reservation. And we must have those options in hand by 2:00 P.M. tomorrow." Of course, we were elated.

Monte turned to me and said, "Roy, you've got a job to do tomorrow morning." I recognized I had quite a responsibility. I had no idea who owned those properties, how many owners I had to deal with, nor if they lived in Tucson or Timbuktu.

Despite the hour, I went to the phone to call Leo Finch, Pima County assessor, in whose office records of property ownership were

kept. I apologized for getting him out of bed at that late hour and explained that something important for Tucson was up. I asked him to
meet me at six the next morning at his office so that I could look up
the ownership of property near the airport. He was nice about being
disturbed in the middle of the night and agreed to meet me. Monte set
up a luncheon at his home for noon the next day for those who were
present that evening. He said, rather ominously, "We'll be waiting for
you to come with the options for that property."

Very early the next morning, I was in my office typing up an option
form to use if and when the property owners were willing to agree to
sell. Then I met Leo Finch.

Fortunately, I found that the property we needed on the eastern
boundary had only one owner, a tallow company that rendered car-
casses of cattle and pigs and produced several by-products. The company had local owners, several of whom I knew. I called the president
of the company and made an appointment to see him at nine. When I
explained the situation, without revealing the name of company wanting the land, the man said they'd sell if they could get their price for
their 1,300-acre parcel, and especially if they could lease it back and
continue their operation for a few years. (So far as I know they are
still operating there.)

He called a meeting of his board of directors for lunch at the Pioneer Hotel that noon. I attended their meeting to explain the situation
and the urgency for an answer. I excused myself for a few minutes to
allow them to make their decision. They put a reasonable price on the
property and signed the option agreement.

We were fortunate that most of the property along the north border of the airport was owned by a wealthy man from the East who
had been living in Tucson for many years and was a friend of mine.
He owned a full section of land, 640 acres. He put a reasonable price
on the property and signed the option. The other two owners of the
balance of the property needed were not quite so easy to locate, but I
was fortunate to find them and both also signed options.

I dashed out to Monte's house in El Encanto Estates and proudly
announced that I had the options from the owners of most of the land
needed. Upon examining the maps of the area and the property optioned, General Eaker said that he was sure "the boss" would be satisfied and that Hughes would be willing to make the proper announcement about coming to Tucson, but he insisted that it be delayed for a
week to ten days.

During that time, General Eaker told me that the company would need at least 10,000 acres near the airport. He asked me to get options on as much land as I could. He and I had maps that we would refer to every evening when I would make my daily reports to him. When I had optioned the 10,000 acres, he said they wanted to obtain yet another 10,000 acres as soon as possible! He sent a company real estate man to Tucson by the name of McLain to work with me. We got along fine. During this time, landowners in Tucson heard about my efforts to buy land and began calling me, offering their properties for sale. After I had 20,000 acres under option, General Eaker said they'd like to have still another 10,000 acres under option, which were not difficult to get, because I wouldn't haggle with the owners over the price if I could obtain a ninety-day option. I finally ended up with 32,000 acres of raw land under option around Tucson. At that point General Eaker said they thought that was enough.

They were at last ready to announce that Howard Hughes would have his company build a large electronics plant in Tucson that would employ at least 5,000 people in high-paying jobs. Hughes also authorized Monte to make a similar announcement through the local media in Tucson. It was still January of 1951, and the decision by Hughes to build this important plant in Tucson had taken fewer than three weeks to make, not counting the behind-the-scenes efforts of Axel Johnson to quietly convince executives of Hughes that Tucson was the place they should be.

Ironically, a few days after the announcement, which included a statement that the Del Webb Company would be the contractor to construct the building, Del called me and said that Howard Hughes had thanked him for the job his people did in making the necessary arrangements for Hughes's negotiators to come to Tucson and obtain the options for the land. But, Del told me, Hughes said he would not pay any commissions for the real estate—he didn't like real estate brokers. I told Del that all of the options were in my name and that I had put up almost $8,000 in option money for some of the properties. Del said something would have to be worked out.

I had become pretty well acquainted with Tex Thornton. When he heard that Howard Hughes had refused to pay the commissions, he remarked that he knew I had worked too hard not to be paid. He said the amount, about $95,000, would be added to Webb's contract for the construction of the building and Webb could then pay me, which was done. That was a lot of money in those days, especially for a fairly new broker.

One further note: One of the last pieces I put under option was a full section of land that Monte Mansfeld had owned for many years. It was located in the foothills on the east side of North Campbell Avenue, along the last mile of the paved road immediately adjoining the Coronado Forest. Monte put a price on it of $105,000, which Hughes eventually paid. Monte had bought it years before for $3 an acre, or less than $2,000 for the entire 640 acres. I understand that one of Tucson's most exclusive and expensive subdivisions is now located on the land, and one- and two-acre lots are selling for $100,000 to $200,000 each. Hughes paid a total of $1.9 million for the 20,000 acres they bought, and eventually sold the land for close to $100 million. Hughes used less than 300 acres of the 20,000 he bought for company purposes—for 400 or 500 houses. He was a shrewd real estate investor and owned the land in his personal estate.

Incidentally, Axel Johnson was appointed manager of the Hughes plant and got to live in Tucson for several years.

Bond Issues of 1965 and Tucson at a Crossroads

THERE HAVE BEEN bond issues proposed to voters over many, many years in the Tucson area. Generally, voters have approved more than they have turned down, but it appears that voters approve or refuse bonds in cycles.

Tucson experienced a considerable increase in population following World War II. By the early 1960s, there was a pent-up need for many things. Schools, roads, and streets; larger wastewater treatment plants; water wells and pipes to distribute water to new and spreading residential areas; and additional police and fire stations, courts, and jails, and other security facilities were badly needed. Yet, in the early 1960s, a bond issue proposed by Tucson Unified School District was defeated. Pima County, likewise, experienced a defeat by voters on a bond issue.

In 1963, the city of Tucson went to the voters with a list of bond proposals. Newsome Holesapple, a prominent and respected real estate agent, and I served as cochairs of the City Bond Committee. We ran what we thought was an intelligent campaign, supporting the bond proposals. However, only one or two of the eight to ten proposals were approved; the rest were handily defeated.

The elected officials, facing large demands from the public, couldn't understand why the voters refused, time after time, to approve the issuing of bonds to satisfy those demands. Businesspeople were very concerned about the failure of the community to provide badly needed improvements. There was no evidence of any particular organized group opposing bond issues, but they were defeated nevertheless.

Lew Davis, a successful businessman, was mayor of Tucson. The city council was made up of respected people who were working well together and not involved in the petty politics evident in more recent years. Still the voters turned down the bond issue that had been recommended by the mayor and council.

One night in November 1964, I got a phone call at home from Mayor Davis, who was a good friend of mine. He asked me to come down to a city council meeting at the city hall. He said they wanted to talk to me. I told him it was after ten o'clock and that I had my pajamas on, but he insisted that I get dressed and come to the meeting anyway. I did.

I was told they were going to propose another bond issue and wanted me to be chairman of a citizens' bond committee to promote its passage. I agreed to take on the task, provided they would appoint the businesspeople I selected to serve on the committee. I told them they could add other people to it but that I didn't want to have a preponderance of political hacks to work with.

The next day, I met with the mayor, the city manager, and their staffs to organize the program and establish dates and deadlines for various phases of the campaign. The bond election date was set for late April 1965.

This was a vital bond program. It made possible Tucson's participation in the national urban renewal movement designed to rejuvenate our inner cities. The city would acquire blocks and blocks of crumbling adobe houses and buildings to make room for the construction of the Community Center, which would include a large sports arena, a music center, a smaller live theater, and a large parking garage. The bonds would also provide financing for a new city hall building; a new police station on South Stone Avenue; several new firehouses and parks; and miles of new streets, water lines, and sewer lines.

Not one person refused an invitation to join the committees that would analyze the issues and then promote the appropriate bonds at the polls. It was apparent to most businesspeople that Tucson simply had to face the fact that we could no longer fail to fund such needed improvements.

We decided to establish a committee to review each of the items for which a specific amount was included in the bond issue. As an example, for a proposed new police station, a special group was appointed to go over the need, the planned building, and the amount requested by the police department. That citizens' committee would spend a great deal of time studying not only the Tucson police department, but law enforcement issues in other cities and what future requirements might be.

This process was followed for each of the bond items. We also enlisted various public relations firms to help publicize the goings-on of these ad hoc committees, which were looking ahead toward at least the next twenty-five years.

It should be pointed out that in 1963, 1964, and 1965, the southwestern part of the United States (including Albuquerque, El Paso, San Diego, Phoenix, and Tucson) was suffering economically while the rest of the nation was prospering. Why that was so has never been explained, but Tucson was fortunate that this was a quiet period of growth that allowed the community a breathing spell and the opportunity to get its house in order for the prosperous period that soon came.

Studies of the needs of the various city departments continued during the early months of 1965, with over 200 men and women participating in the process. The citizens' committees were finding the requests for the expenditures justified. Every week, the press ran articles reporting those findings to the community. The end result was approval of each of the bond proposals.

Soon afterward, the Pima County Board of Supervisors approached our committee and asked us to study *their* needs and support their bond issue for badly needed facilities. Our committee reorganized and accepted the request. We were successful in that campaign, too.

The principal improvements financed with those bond funds were the three high-rise buildings presently housing the offices of the board of supervisors (and of many other county departments and agencies), the building containing the Pima County court system, and the building known as the County Morgue. They comprise the core of the county's and city's government center today. Tucson's downtown was changed forever.

Also financed by that county bond issue was a new and enlarged wastewater treatment plant, which has been serving the community for many years, and land for the present downtown Holiday Inn.

Tucson Unified School District No. 1 soon approached us and asked for our support for the bonds *they* needed to develop new schools and rejuvenate some of the older buildings. Once again, our committee accepted the invitation, went through the process, and eventually supported the school bond program. It, too, was approved by the voters.

This whole series of events was a prime example of a community's business and professional men and women organizing themselves and deciding that it was absolutely essential that voters and taxpayers support the decisions of their elected officials to move Tucson forward. The city was at a crossroads and took the high road to provide things it needed and has been using for over thirty years. Life in the Old Pueblo has been better because of those actions taken in the mid-1960s.

Historical Events That Helped Shape Tucson

IN LOOKING BACK through the years of this century for important things that occurred here and which have had an effect on what our community has become, I think we should consider not only what happened locally but also the impact national and international events have had on Tucson. I'd like to identify the city's historical milestones during this century, as well as some important events that have had substantial bearing on our community but which do not qualify as milestones. This is one man's opinion: mine.

As the Old Pueblo entered this century it was a very small, dusty town of some 7,500 souls who survived rugged living conditions and who earned meager incomes.

Nothing happened during the first twenty years of this century that could qualify as a milestone in Tucson's history, although during the second decade some events occurred that had an important impact on the community's morals.

Gambling, prostitution, and the sale of alcoholic beverages were outlawed, all of which doubtless improved the image of the Old Pueblo as a more civilized place than it had been previously considered to be. Arizona became the nation's forty-eighth state, but that actually didn't do much for Tucson immediately. World War I occurred from 1914 to 1918, but it did not have nearly the lasting effect on Tucson that World War II had in the '40s.

During the first twenty years of this century Tucson experienced some favorable economic benefits from an expanding University of Arizona. The division headquarters of the Southern Pacific Railroad was Tucson's largest employer, and the coming of the El Paso & Southwestern railroad in 1915 provided a hefty boost to the city's economy. The home office of the Southern Pacific Railroad de México was also located here and provided employment for quite a few office workers.

One of the most important sources of money for the community was the pockets of health seekers from all over the nation, who had heard that the climate was especially good for those suffering from tuberculosis. Several sanatoriums operated here, catering to those known as TBs, or "lungers." Soon after World War II the Veterans Bureau established a hospital here on the grounds of the former Pastime Park, a recreational facility on Oracle Road some five miles north of the city, but it was a relatively small operation for which only wood frame buildings were constructed.

In 1910 Tucson's population was approximately 13,000, which made it the largest city in Arizona. Phoenix had only 10,000 or so people.

When the population figures for 1920 were released, Tucsonans were shocked to learn that whereas the population here had increased to 20,292, Phoenix had grown to over 29,000!

The great jump in population in the Valley of the Sun occurred as a result of several things. Phoenix's increase in importance as a result of its being a state capital, instead of a territorial one, was one factor. The establishment of several federal agencies there, which created employment for many people, was another. But more important was the development of Roosevelt Dam and the construction of the canal system. That project brought water to thousands of acres of desert land around Phoenix, which converted the valley into an important farming community.

Tucson businessmen, most of whom were members of the Tucson

Chamber of Commerce and strong boosters of their town, did not take such a "catastrophic" event lying down. They were determined that Tucson could again become the premiere city in Arizona. But how?

That question brought all kinds of answers. After a year or so of soul-searching, the powers of that time agreed that Tucson could and should become a tourist and health center. Several months of meetings selling the idea to the business community and elected officials followed. It was finally decided that an organization separate from the Chamber of Commerce should be established to advertise that Tucson had the most healthful climate in North America. So the Tucson Sunshine Climate Club was formed to tell the world how wonderful Tucson was for both tourists and health seekers.

The city and the county provided money to pay for the advertisements that were placed in national magazines such as the *National Geographic,* the *American Medical Journal, Time,* and a few others. The business community provided the money to cover operating expenses, including the production of brochures and mailing costs.

The well-known national advertising agency, McCann-Erickson, handled the account and helped develop methods to evaluate the effectiveness of various publications. Generally, the business community was satisfied that its future was tied closely to the tourist and health business.

It soon became apparent that the existing hotels did not provide the kind of accommodations that the high-quality visitors coming to the Old Pueblo demanded. A few ranchers began to accept winter visitors, but there still was a demand for better hotel facilities.

Tucson business leaders such as Monte Mansfeld, Hi Corbett, Jesse James, Harold Steinfeld, John Reilly, and many others decided that a new resort hotel should be built here. They put on a fundraising campaign and sold stock to business and professional men. With those funds, and others resulting from a mortgage on the land and building, they were able to finance the construction of the El Conquistador Hotel on East Broadway, where the El Con shopping center is located today. The site was far out on the east side, and the hotel, when completed, could be seen for miles in any direction. The hotel contained over 200 rooms and suites, as well as all the other accoutrements demanded by wealthy visitors.

In a few years dozens and dozens of guest ranches and other smaller inns and lodges were developed here. About that time the Desert Sanatorium, which offered first-class health facilities to visitors, was built. It later was converted to a community hospital and became the Tucson Medical Center.

This drive for Tucson to become a major tourist and health center began in the 1920 to 1922 period, when the community's leaders recognized that this city could not become a farming community like Phoenix, nor an industrial center, because it lacked the natural resources.

So I believe that decision was one that set the course for Tucson in that era and continues today, as the city continues to fulfill its role as a tourist and health center. Further development of that concept will occur in the years ahead.

Milestone number one for Tucson in the twentieth century, then, was its decision to become a tourist and health Center.

MILESTONE NUMBER TWO occurred around the midpoint of the 1930s, during the Depression. Air-conditioning became a fact of life with the development of the "swamp cooler," which enabled every household and small business to cool their premises to comfortable levels at reasonable costs. No longer did nearly everyone plan to someday move away and escape the horrible heat that made life almost unbearable in the summer. In fact, the development of reasonably priced air-conditioning was a milestone not only for Tucson but also for all communities located in the southwestern states.

Milestone number two for Tucson during this century was the availability of air cooling for the majority of people.

THE NEXT IMPORTANT milestone in Tucson's history during the current century occurred in the latter part of the 1930s, and the war years of the 1940s.

Although the United States was not officially involved in the turmoil occurring in Europe after Hitler came to power in Germany, most Americans' sympathies lay with their traditional allies: England, France, and Belgium. And as negotiations went on between Hitler and the leaders of England and France, it was apparent to most observers that nothing less than war was going to stop Hitler from controlling every country in Europe.

American industry was most willing to cooperate with the Roosevelt administration in producing guns, tanks, airplanes, and other war equipment to be sold to European nations preparing for war. In fact, most people were happy to see our nation get back to work after many years of economic depression.

This nationwide activity affected Tucson as it did most cities. Factories to build war equipment were going up across the country. Tucson was anxious to get in on the action, and the Chamber of Commerce began plans to attract either a factory or some kind of a military base.

Monte Mansfeld, who was president of the chamber and also chairman of the Tucson Airport Commission, was sent to Washington to accomplish that. Working with Senator Carl Hayden and other contacts, Monte returned to Tucson with promises of a large air base, which became today's Davis-Monthan field.

The community was delighted. Monte Mansfeld was the man of the hour.

The U.S. Army Air Corps would take over the then-existing Tucson airport, which would have to be moved to another site. The city of Tucson acquired several hundred acres of raw land south of town and began the development of the Tucson Municipal Airport, which was later leased to the newly created Tucson Airport Authority.

The government soon began construction and development of Davis-Monthan field, and millions of dollars began to flow into our local economy.

Soon after that, other military operations began to move into our city, bringing money and people to the Old Pueblo. The impact of the turmoil in Europe was definitely being felt here.

The third important milestone of Tucson's history in the twentieth century was beginning to take form. It continued during the years that our nation was at war. Thousands of young men and women were exposed to Tucson's weather and its beautiful desert setting. Later, many returned to visit or to live here.

A pattern of rapid growth was established for both Tucson and Phoenix. Each community began to abandon its principal economic reliance on cotton, copper, and cattle.

The local tourist business boomed during the war years because people could no longer travel abroad. Tucson had 112 guest ranches within 50 miles, and 8 important private schools, which attracted youngsters from wealthy families in the Midwest and on the East Coast.

When the war ended, there was a great pent-up demand for all the kinds of buildings that could not be constructed during the war, especially homes. The construction boom that followed immediately was part of the historic event that formed this milestone.

Milestone number three for Tucson in the twentieth century was World War II.

THE NEXT IMPORTANT milestone occurred in 1951, when the Hughes Company (now Raytheon) built its large electronics plant here.

At that time Tucson was no longer booming from its activities during the war years. Although there was considerable military training at Davis-Monthan, Marana Field, and Fort Huachuca, as well as modification of military planes at the Convair plant, the community had resumed its traditional role of a steadily growing college town catering to tourists and health seekers.

The arrival of the Hughes plant created an unparalleled level of excitement throughout the community. Never had such a large manufacturing company been located here. Home builders recognized the upcoming need for housing and revved up their operations. Land values jumped overnight with the news that Howard Hughes had purchased some 20,000 acres of desert land.

Rumors that other electronic companies would be following Hughes to the Old Pueblo elevated expectations of future prosperity here to unheard of heights.

The "City Fathers," together with business leaders, stepped forward and set in progress a wave of public works, which included paving of many streets and roads, construction of school buildings, extension of water and sewer lines, and other municipal improvements.

Hughes triggered a pattern that continued during the balance of the 1950s, which proved to be one of Tucson's most dramatic growth periods

The city would never be the same. There can be little question that the coming of Hughes to Tucson was truly one of the city's most important milestones. So milestone number four for Tucson was the construction of the Hughes plant, which made Tucson part of the world of electronics in 1951.

THE NEXT HISTORICAL milestone for Tucson was the tragic fire at the Pioneer Hotel in late December 1970.

At the 1948 Pioneer Hotel retirement party of J. C. Penney's manager, Matt Mansfield (seated), the movers and shakers of Tucson's business and civic community gather. *Left to right* Jim Ewing, Sam Seeney, Max Pooler, Aaron Levy, Roy, Hi Corbett, Jack Proctor, Ed Goyette, George Stonecypher, Ralph Bilby, Harold Steinfeld, Alex Jacome, Jack J. O'Dowd, Andy Martin, Jim Houston, and one faceless guy. *Reginald Russell photo.*

The fire destroyed the hotel and took the lives of twenty-eight people. But that fire did something else to the community. For several years prior to that, Tucson's downtown area had begun to suffer from the flight of important retail stores to outlying shopping centers.

But the heart of the city was still considered to be downtown. The Pioneer Hotel was the heart of that heart, as much as any one place could be. The largest Rotary and Kiwanis Clubs in the city met there weekly, as did other civic organizations, attracting important people from throughout the community for perhaps their only trip downtown during the week.

The Pioneer was also the meeting place for shoppers or diners before or after shopping trips to the few stores remaining in the downtown area.

When fire destroyed the Pioneer, all that ended. The fire removed the last and most important symbol of a strong downtown. It heralded the end of Tucson's being different from other cities that had experienced massive movement out of their downtowns to the suburban shopping centers, office complexes, hotels, restaurants, cinemas, and other recreational facilities.

Tucson's downtown never recovered from the loss of its heart: the Pioneer Hotel. So Tucson's fifth milestone was the Pioneer Hotel fire.

THE NEXT MILESTONE occurred when the ownership of the *Arizona Daily Star* and the *Tucson Citizen* passed from local families to national newspaper companies.

The purchaser of the *Star,* the St. Louis–based Pulitzer company, owns many other newspapers, as well as radio and television stations. The company is controlled by members of the Pulitzer family. One member of that family moved to Tucson soon after the purchase. It was hoped that the family would become active in community affairs, which unfortunately did not happen.

After a short time the Pulitzer family moved out of the Old Pueblo, leaving the operation of the *Star* in the hands of its employees, many of whom are longtime Tucsonans.

For several decades the *Star* had been owned and operated by the William Mathews and the Ralph Ellinwood families, both of whom lived here and depended on the success of the paper for their livelihood.

Bill Mathews was editor of the *Star* and played a very active role in everything that went on here and, for that matter, what went on in Arizona. He was a fearless editor who did not hesitate to be critical of people in high places if he felt they were doing something that would be harmful to his town or state.

Many people did not like or agree with him, but they all respected him, especially politicians and elected officials. He owned a responsible, committed newspaper that most thoughtful people read, not only in Tucson but also in Phoenix.

He gave himself to causes he felt were worthwhile and important to his city. As an example, when the Arizona legislature refused to provide funding for the first phases of the establishment of the Arizona Medical School, despite the fact that an independent study clearly stated that a medical school was needed in Arizona, and that the University of Arizona, not Arizona State, was where the medical school should be located, he did something about it.

He organized a committee and chaired a campaign to raise the $3 million needed to kick off the development of the new school. This money, together with the traditional 3 to 1 matching funds from the federal Hill-Burton assistance for medical facilities, would provide the $9 million needed to create the first element of the new school in Tucson.

Mathews and his committee did raise the $3 million, and the medical school became a reality, largely as a result of Bill Mathews's dedication to his community. He provided the kind of leadership that has been lacking here since the sale of the Tucson newspapers.

When Mathews died, and the *Star* and *Citizen* later fell into the ownership of people who did not live here or have the interest of the community as their number one priority, Tucson suffered a great loss, primarily in *leadership,* backed up by a powerful voice, which is still hugely missed here today.

Soon after the *Star* was sold, the evening paper, the *Tucson Citizen,* was sold to another large company, the Gannett Publishing Company, which owns many other newspapers throughout the nation.

Tucson was left without a locally owned daily newspaper, and although the people employed by these out-of-town owners live here now, have taken their places in the community, and are active in its affairs, it just is not the same as when a local editor had the guts to take on the biggest of bigwigs and fight for what he thought was best for Tucson, without concern for the impact on the bottom line or on his job.

I'm certain that my friends at both of the daily newspapers will disagree with this premise, so to be fair about it I should concede that newspapers everywhere have lost much of their power to the electronic media, a fact that would hamper any local editor.

Tucson's sixth milestone was, nonetheless, the sale of the two local dailies to large corporations headquartered elsewhere.

THE NEXT THING that had a lasting effect on the community was a serious mistake made by the Tucson City Council, and more particularly by one councilman, who cast the deciding vote to turn down a request by the Motorola Company to rezone a property it had an option to buy on the near northwest side, where it planned to build a large electronics plant. That company has been the largest employer in Arizona for many years, employing over 20,000 in the valley around Phoenix. The number of people who would have been employed in the high-paying Tucson plant would have numbered between 4,000 and 5,000.

Because Tucson turned Motorola down, the company has built numerous plants in the Phoenix area, in and around Austin, Texas, and in quite a few other places that did not have anything to offer that Tucson couldn't provide, except a willingness to welcome them as a very valuable asset to the community. I have been told by one of Motorola's highest executives that they never have been turned down by any other community and will never consider Tucson again as a site for one of their plants.

I am certain that if Motorola had been welcomed to Tucson, it, along with Hughes, would have built one or more plants here, and would have assured this community's status as a good place for other desirable electronics plants to locate. The Old Pueblo would have become a powerhouse in the field of electronics. The loss is enormous.

The seventh milestone for Tucson was the city's blind refusal to provide a site for the Motorola Company.

DURING THE PAST ten years Tucson's growth has not been very rapid. In fact, between 1989 and 1994, the city's rate of growth was definitely below the long-term pattern established over many years, having dropped to between 1 and 2 percent. Consequently, there have been many hard-pressed businesspeople here, and the rate of bankruptcies has increased considerably. In my opinion that serious downturn in our economy ironically triggered the establishment and financial support for the next Tucson milestone. Local business leaders and elected officials recognized the need for history-making action to do something to bring the economy back to good health.

Although that next milestone for Tucson, then, was not an event as easily identifiable as some others, I believe that the date that the Greater Tucson Economic Council was formed is a signal one in Tucson's economic history. The mere fact that the elected officials at both the city and county levels recognize the importance of contributing substantial public funds to the endeavor of inviting industrial companies to bring jobs to the community is an important achievement.

GTEC combines public efforts with those of the business community in a program that presents Tucson to the rest of the world as a place that offers many advantages to companies seeking a place with a good labor force, a pleasant and healthful environment, access to a great research university, and opportunities to operate a profitable business.

So the formation of Greater Tucson Economic Council is the city's milestone number eight in the twentieth century.

CLEARLY, OTHER FACTORS, such as the development of the University's many outstanding programs, including the Arizona Health Sciences Center, have played an important part in Tucson's social and economic development. But none of these has risen to the level of a true milestone. I might point out that I am in a unique position to make the above observations, having been an attentive student of, and participant in, Tucson's history during most of this century. Naturally, I have my biases—but I don't know anyone who doesn't, nor can I think of anyone else so closely connected to the Tucson scene for so long who is still around. I certainly don't claim to be infallible, so help yourself to being critical and selecting your own milestones. It's easier and less hazardous to your health than having gallstones.

Index

Note: Page numbers in italics indicate a photograph of subject on that page.

From Cowtown to Desert Metropolis
was set in 10.5/13 Sabon
with Gill Sans display.
The designer was Harrison Shaffer,
and the text was typeset by
TypeWorks in Tucson, Arizona.
The books were printed and bound
by Thomson-Shore in Ann Arbor,
Michigan. The project editor was
Sonya Manes of Elizabeth Shaw
Editorial & Publishing Services.